The [...] Plan for Empaths & HSPs –

The Easy Permanent Path to Emotional Freedom, Weight-Loss, Health and Happiness!

Contents

Introduction

1. Why Does Diet Have to Do with Anything?   01
2. What is all The Fuss with Wheat?   12
3. Oh Sugar   28
4. Pleasure or Pain   36
5. Soothe the Seat of Emotions   48
6. Nature's Elixir   59
7. Fundamentals of Exercise   64
8. Mind Control   72
9. What to Expect   79
10. Gluten and Food Intolerance   89
11. 4-Week Elimination   97
12. Wheat and Sugar-Free Cooking   108
13. Recipes   118
14 Let Nature Heal You   259
15. 8 Ways to Stop Overwhelm   265
16. 10 Essential Oils to Re-Balance   269
17. Conclusion   272

Introduction

In 2012, I stumbled across an online interview with the American cardiologist, Dr William Davies, that changed my life as an Empath. The strange thing was the interview had nothing to do with the traits of the Sensitive, it was about modern wheat!

Dr Davies explained how wheat has been genetically altered and how this change has led to the obesity, diabetes and depression epidemics sweeping the globe. Having always had problems with my weight, like many Sensitive people do, his claims immediately caught my attention. It was on the strength of his convictions that I decided to try wheat elimination.

I gave myself a month; telling myself if I saw no change, I could go back to eating wheat. But within that time some remarkable changes happened: My hyperacidity, which caused me a great deal of stomach pain, disappeared, my appetite significantly reduced, and I felt healthier and happier. Yet, what I was most surprised at was how its elimination affected my Sensitivities.

Those which I had considered to be my "negative Empath traits" were having less impact. Being in public places or around certain people were not causing the typical crushing overwhelm. I could still feel the energy of others, but it did not 'break' me in the usual way. And my intuition was becoming stronger. That was just the start of some remarkable changes.

As the months came and went, I knew I was doing something transformational. People started to comment on my weight-loss and how well I looked, they wanted to know what I was doing differently. I was fascinated by the changes I saw unfold within myself. But what I was most astounded by, and not expecting at all, was how these simple alterations to my diet helped me as an Empath. I was stunned that what I consumed had such a profound effect. I assumed, like many of you do, that most of what I experienced emotionally was down to being a Sensitive person, living in the midst of a chaotic world. I discovered my 'negative traits' had all been heightened and exaggerated by what I was eating. And if this was how wheat affected my Sensitive characteristics, I was curious to find out how other foods shaped them.

I came to understand that although I would always be in tune with the energy of other people, I was not supposed to be constantly taken down by them. But because my body and mind had been weakened by what I was eating, I could not handle what I was feeling as an Empath. My diet had been scrambling my inner-signals, which had a detrimental impact on my Sensitivities. I wanted to know why. And this led to further research into how drug-like foods affect those of us who are Sensitive.

Since then my life has continued to transform in many positive ways. As an Empath, I still get peopled and drained by being around certain others and I still get overstimulated, but at normal levels. The steps I take to prevent or reduce overwhelm now work, and when I am out-of-balance, I can zone in on the exact cause, whether it be food, people or the environment.

Having witnessed first-hand the amazing changes that

happen by making alterations to the diet, I want to pass this knowledge on. Life as an Empath or HSP already comes with enough challenges. We should not be taken down by our food, nor do we have to be.

This eating plan has been devised and written with the intention of reshaping your life as a Sensitive. By following the advice within these pages, you can see a transformation in your emotional health, stress levels, appearance, weight, all over wellbeing and happiness.

If you are Sensitive, then this book is for you!

I use the term "**Sensitive**" to describe the Empath or Highly Sensitive Person. In other words: those who possess heightened senses, those who react to their environment, emotions and energy of other people, and those who have a highly developed sense of awareness, intuition, a need for solitude and quiet.

As a self-proclaimed Empath, introvert and HSP, I have studied the traits of the Sensitive for many years in a bid to find balance and heal myself. After much research and self-trials, I know that our diet plays an integral part in how we show up in the world. And until we make adjustments to what we eat, we will never find true balance. This book is an accumulation of years' study into nutrition, holistic health and healing, and a lifetime of being an Empath.

Suffer No More

Too many Sensitive people are suffering without understanding why. My aim is to assist you in making the necessary changes, so you too can start living the brilliant life you were born to live! Now is the time for you to get back in control. Take the plunge and start making the changes you know will transform your life as a Sensitive!

How to use this book?

For easier navigation I have split this book into 3 sections.

Section 1 Gives you the lowdown on how your diet has impacted your Sensitive traits. It gives you the ways to make incredible changes through diet, supplementation and more.

Section 2 Contains recipes and meal ideas. It is common when changing the diet to not know where to start with meal ideas. This section is designed to help you with that. It won't take long before you find your feet and become a whizz in the wheat-free kitchen.

Section 3 A guide to staying grounded and balance. We all have off days, even after changing the diet. This section gives you the tools to stay in balance as a Sensitive even when you have had the most stressful or overwhelming days.

Section 1

1

What Does Diet Have to Do with Anything?

Diet has more impact on the negative aspects of being Sensitive than you may imagine. So much so, a book is needed to explain why.

We often blame our "Sensitivity stress" for all our emotional upheavals and inability to spend time around people, but many of our weaknesses begin with the food we put into our mouth. Certain foods create havoc with our emotional wellbeing and the sooner we become aware of this, the sooner we can make changes. The point of this book isn't about going on a diet, feeling deprived or hungry, it's about removing drug-like foods from your life and seeing the miraculous changes that happen after. You never need to feel deprived again. Nor do you need to feel mentally dependent on any food.

The majority of Sensitive people only attempt to change their diet, as a last resort, after trying everything else. We don't always want to know how destructive drug-like

1

foods are to our emotional health because they have such a powerful mental hold. Changing the diet may seem like one of the hardest things to do, but it really isn't. Only our thoughts and addictions make the notion a torturous idea.

Because the body weakens with age, we have to put more effort into finding balance as we get older. What we could happily consume in our twenties, can act as poison in our forties. Eating foods that weaken the body and mind cause more and more damage with each passing year. Drug-like processed foods not only deplete the body but affect our hormones and endocrine glands, lower our moods and, in some cases, cause severe mental disorders. I could not have imagined what an impact diet has to our emotional health or the way we pick up and process emotions belonging to others, had I not witnessed it first-hand. Our eating patterns also determine the way we interpret stress.

Whether Sensitive or not, our body and mind was designed to handle stress on many levels. In the past, stress may have come from being in life-threatening situations or simply not knowing where our next meal was coming from. Stress has been part of our everyday lives for eons. Emotional and energetic stress is part of the human experience and is not supposed to make life a living hell. But because the body is in such a weakened state, from the toxic-food we consume, any type of stress eventually becomes debilitating, affecting our brain, thoughts, health and wellbeing.

By eating foods that have a drug-like effect on the brain, life can become an arduous, tormenting task instead of the intriguing satisfying journey it should be. The cornerstone to transformation involves removing two specific foods. These foods act like narcotics and have been proven to light up the opiate receptors of the brain worse than heroin. They cause emotional and energetic challenges and the sooner they are eliminated the better. These two foods are wheat and refined sugar.

The emotional overwhelm endured by those of us with a Sensitive nature can be distressing. It makes living in the world difficult. But many of our emotional responses are ignited and worsened by these two everyday foods. The good news is, these responses are quickly dialed down by the elimination of wheat and sugar and this book will show you how this can be done easily and effortlessly!

As humans we differ greatly and as Sensitives, our imbalances are no different. But the steps laid out in this book apply to everyone and those who follow them can see their lives transform in the most positive way.

For some, the idea of making changes to the diet can seem like a daunting task. But don't worry, know that what is presented in this eating plan can reshape your life in ways you may not have imagined, and any worries you may have had will be pushed aside once you experience these 'side-effects'.

Fail to Prepare

There is a saying that '*if you fail to prepare, then you should prepare to fail*'. This is relevant when making any lifestyle changes, but no more so than when it comes to the diet. If you want to see positive transformations in your life, you have to make changes and this involves preparation. But first you need to understand why these lifestyle adjustments are so important. Knowledge is power. When you know the steps and why you are taking them, you are already half-way to transformation. This book gives you the steps and the information. From one Sensitive to another.

There is another old saying that is apt here: '*The proof is in the pudding*'. If you follow the plan, laid out within these pages, it won't take long before you see for yourself how food has been impacting your emotional and physical wellbeing. For some, it can take as little as two weeks before noticing big differences. For others it takes less time or longer. But you will see a change.

So, what can you expect to see from this eating plan? Weight-loss (if needed), better health, a significant increase in happiness, reduced brain-fog, increased energy, the ability to disengage from negative energy, greatly improved digestive health, decreased stress, great skin, age-reversal, emotional freedom and much more.

Over the years, many of you have been intuitively poked and prodded to pay attention to your diet. Those nagging feelings that you need to make changes, probably bought you to this book, which is your guide to making them happen.

If you want to see incredible changes in your life, then change your diet... Simple!

Modern diets and lifestyles have taken too many Sensitive people down without them knowing. Most have no idea how food hinders their happiness, or how removing wheat and sugar can transform their emotional health. This is what I am on a mission to change. The root-cause of many health problems seen in both body and mind is what we feed on. The low-fat, high-wheat/sugar and chemical laden diets we have been consuming these past thirty years has turned us into low-

4

level-thinking zombies. Which has contributed to stress, depression and countless other health conditions. In those of us who are Sensitive, poor diet has contributed to creating heightened emotions, depressive tendencies, being overly sensitive and an inability to function when around certain others. Until we address the diet and remove foods responsible for causing emotional and physical chaos, we will not find the peaceful state we all strive for.

The physical ailments, debilitating feelings and disorientation many experience (Sensitive or not), are often blamed on ascension symptoms, work stress, negative people and more. But, believe me, they are not all caused by the above. A good number of adverse reactions within the mind and body are directly impacted by what we feed on. Eating foods that act like narcotics or that which the body can no longer tolerate, has a massive antagonistic influence and plays havoc with the Sensitive person's traits. Only when we clean up our diet, do we understand just how much drug-like food impacts our health, spiritual progress and happiness. Wheat and refined sugar have been scientifically proven to have a drug-effect on the brain. These effects create addictive behaviors, mood swings, unhappiness and depression, and disrupt the hormones natural cycle. The Sensitive are already vulnerable to hormonal imbalances and this is another reason it is essential to address the diet.

If we put poison into the body, in the form of toxic food, it will not matter if we sit for hours in meditation, perform yoga or other exercise each day, because no amount of spiritual practice will bring balance. We may believe we are eating a perfectly healthy diet, with lots of so-called 'healthy wholegrains' but as you read on it will become glaringly obvious how misinformed we have all been.

Addictive Foods

If you want to know the foods that cause the worst damage to the mind, body and spirit, and that which you most need to eliminate, it is that which you think you cannot live without. Most specialists working in this field agree: if you resist giving up certain foods it is likely you are addicted or intolerant to them. I guarantee that if you include wheat or refined sugar in your diet, you will not want to give them up.

Natural, healthy food should not create an addiction nor make us want to gorge. Food is our fuel. And although we should be able to enjoy our sustenance, our life should not be controlled by it. When we overeat, we often tell ourselves we are just being greedy, weak and controlled by overconsumption, when it is more likely the drug-like foods enticing the brain into binge-eating. Addictive foods, coupled with an out-of-balance body, create disharmony in the Sensitive person's mental and physical health. So much so, it can create complete imbalance and, in some cases, neurotic behavior. Anything that is addictive does not and will never agree with the body's delicate chemistry. The two foods pivotal for creating imbalance are wheat and refined sugar (which are in all processed foods). If you want to see transformation happen, then they have to be eliminated completely. And it is much easier to do than you might think.

Food That Acts Like Opiate Drugs

Depending on the Sensitivity of a person will depend on the speed which disorders show up when consuming damaging foods. High reactive people get sicker sooner than those who feel less and have a thicker skin.

Emotional upset and stress weaken the body, but foods that act like drugs and affect hormonal balance, eventually debilitate the mind and can cause irrational or phobic attitudes. You may be able to eat these foods for ten to twenty years before you see the harm they cause. But believe me, the damage eventually shows up as an imbalance. Once symptoms appear, they gradually get worse over time. We have to be vigilant about changing our diet and removing damaging foods.

All drug-like foods not only create addiction but play havoc with the Sensitive person's body chemistry. They ramp up negative traits and tone down the more positive; making it difficult to operate in the world. Because these drug-like foods affect the opioid receptors in the brain, making them hyperactive, it can result in an inability to experience pleasure, and causes a sense of being cut off from true happiness. If you consume anything addictive, you will not want to give them up and will likely get angry at the notion. But by the time you have read this book, you will have a greater idea of what impact they have on your life and, I hope, you will be itching to eliminate them.

The process of taking back your power is done in steps. When removing drug-like foods it should be done with awareness, because anything drug-like creates withdrawal symptoms within the first week or two after elimination. I cover this subject and offer ways to make withdrawal more comfortable later on. Giving up wheat and refined sugar at the same time makes sense because where there is one there will often be the other. It is only when you give them both up permanently that you can see what effect they had on your health and happiness.

Overcoming Addictions

When it comes to addictions, many are unaware they have an addiction to wheat or sugar. I've heard many people say 'I don't have a problem. I hardly have any wheat because I don't eat much bread.' But when I question them further, I find they eat pasta, crackers, biscuits, couscous or pastries on a daily basis... that's a lot of wheat (and sugar!).

It is true, most are unaware how out-of-balance their body is, or how this reflects in their Sensitivities, emotional health and overall wellbeing. Creating a strong, healthy body is essential if we want to find complete balance. We really are what we eat. It may seem tedious to be told the importance of improving diet, but it is an essential component to finding balance as a Sensitive person. If we don't eliminate drug-like foods our bodies will just become more and more out-of-balance. Eating food that debilitates the body and mind will take everyone down, and not just the Sensitive.

It is widely believed that if there is no ill-effect shortly after eating a certain food it is safe to consume. This is not true. Adverse food reactions may not show up in the body or mind for up to forty-eight hours after consumption. And even then, the symptoms can seem minor. Drug-like, processed food, filled with chemicals, and foods to which we are intolerant, not only deplete the body but affect our hormones and endocrine glands, lower our moods and, in some cases, cause severe mental disorders.

It is essential that anyone who is Sensitive gets to grip with their diet. Whatever goes into the body can affect the mind. Wheat and sugar being the worst offenders.

Poor food choices heighten all negative emotional responses and cause unnecessary heartache. Here are just some of the reactions certain foods can cause:

- Paranoia
- Increased emotional sensitivities
- Depression and low moods
- Mood swings
- Overreacting to other people's energy
- Irrational fears and phobias
- Excessive introversion
- Disruption in hormones

Our intuition is always at work, behind the scenes, trying to get our attention about how to care for our-self. But, too often, these promptings go unnoticed for the simple reason we are unaware of their importance. The quiet voice of our inner-guardian is always guiding us. Foods that don't agree with our genetic codes are mostly the ones we become addicted to and are destructive to our wellbeing. When our intuition wants to make us aware of much needed changes, the subject keeps popping into the mind. You may find yourself being drawn to certain websites, books or magazines, that contain information on nutritional health and wellbeing. For example: you may have had thoughts about eliminating refined sugar, and when you walk past a newsstand, you notice all the magazines with articles relating to sugar elimination, you may go into a bookshop and the books that jump out at you all relate to sugar-free lifestyles, or when surfing the internet, you come across posts on the hazards of consuming refined sugar. These little pointers are your intuition's way of getting your attention and it is sensible to listen.

Most already have an inkling of what they should or shouldn't consume to stay healthy, because our inner Knowing is constantly talking to us. Those nagging feelings, that something is not a fit, is the intuition or higher-self at work trying to get our attention. But, as humans, we have a weakness for the forbidden and don't always want to listen to our inner-guidance's recommendations.

If you want to see real magic happen, change your diet and get rid of what holds you back!

We often tell ourselves the reason we don't progress is because we are not confident, or because we fear change or failure. But we have to ask the question why do we feel that way? Oddly enough, many of the insecurities and fears we have, are born from chemical reactions within the body that are caused or worsened by the foods we eat.

Once you embark on the journey of self-healing through changing the diet and re-balancing the mind, you will be astounded at how your life shifts gears. Your happiness increases, your energy levels rise, your sense of purpose becomes defined, and much more. Yes, all from making some simple changes to your diet!

If we want to see life transformations, then we have to work at making changes. I guarantee your mind will tell you otherwise, but the easiest way to experience this transformation is by overhauling the diet. Consuming drug-like foods such as wheat and sugar, or foods that do not agree with one's body chemistry, heighten emotional reactions. The longer they stay in the diet the more damage they cause. Only when they have been eliminated completely, can you see how they affected both your physical and emotional health.

I have devised a four-week plan to help you eliminate wheat and sugar (on page 102). if you are going to get the maximum benefit from this book it is super-important you follow it. The plan not only shows you how to stay clear of these toxic foods, but guides you through the best ways to eat for a happy, healthy life! But for now, we'll take a closer look at these drug-like staples and why they have taken so many people down. If being asked to remove them, you deserve to know why.

2

What is all The Fuss with Wheat?

The Grain Secretly Poisoning You

You would have to live deep underground to not have heard about the amazing transformations people are having after eliminating wheat, and not just the Sensitive folk. It is shameful that it has taken so long to come to light how detrimental wheat is for the body and mind.

You may ask, why now? People have been eating wheat for years, haven't they? Yes, but wheat is not what it used to be. It has been genetically altered, to make it more resilient to weather and bugs. These changes have seemingly made it destructive to our health. Since the mid-eighties we have been eating a hybridized version of the toxic crop. Which also coincides with the rise in obesity, depression and diabetes.

Although wholegrain modern wheat is hailed as a health food, it acts like a narcotic and has been scientifically proven to have a drug-like effect on the brain. This is because when wheat was genetically altered, its protein

12

structure was changed. Now, when digested, wheat breaks down into many small proteins that can cross the blood-brain barrier. These tiny proteins attach themselves to the opiate receptors in the brain. This has the effect of a narcotic but without the 'pleasurable' high.

It has also been scientifically proven that wheat encourages overeating and triggers or worsens mental illness. For those who are Sensitive, wheat may heighten their addictive personality, their emotional state and impacts their brain chemistry.

Mind-Altering Food

Wheat has the ability to alter our perception and natural instincts. Not only affecting how much we eat, but what we eat. It switches off our dietary intuition, designed to protect us from choosing foods and substances damaging to our health. If you include it in your diet, then wheat is controlling you more than you could ever know, and not just in your nutritional choices. It may play a part in other addictive behaviors and is linked to controlling moods; which is bad news for those who are Sensitive. Until you take it out of your diet completely, then and only then will you see how it ruled your mind, moods and weight.

Being 'highly reactive', Sensitive people react more to drug-like foods, such as wheat. Most drugs and alcohol have a low energy and bring the Sensitive person down, fast. Wheat is not classed as a drug but it very much acts like one, therefore carries the same signature. You may not eat bread, but you could still consume lots of wheat. It is hidden in many foods for the reason it keeps us controlled and needing to devour more.

13

Drug-Like Action of Wheat

When I explain to others the remarkable changes that happened in my life, just by eliminating wheat, I see their eyes glaze over. I can feel them go within themselves. Some even get argumentative or angry about the subject. I understand they do not want to hear the benefits of wheat elimination because they do not want to give it up. They do not comprehend that being like a drug, they are addicted to wheat, and it is actually their addiction creating the resistance. If told eliminating apples would turn their life around, most wouldn't think twice about ditching them... because apples aren't addictive.

You may have so far believed that your moods and wellbeing have been affected by being unhappy in your home life, stressed in your work, by spending too much time around negative people, or by picking up painful emotions from others, and yes, many problems are caused by the above. But Sensitive traits are also worsened by certain foods.

I found lots of my 'emotional stuff' was caused or worsened by wheat proteins. I only discovered this once they were out of my system. When I eliminated wheat, my thoughts gained clarity and the dark cloud that often lingered over me, lifted. I appreciate not everyone will have the same life-changes I did, or the thousands of others who also eliminated wheat, but by its elimination you will very likely see your life as a Sensitive turn around! Life simply gets better.

Giving up wheat was the catalyst for a total transformation for me. By its removal, I could also see how other foods were affecting my health. Within a year of elimination, I had completely changed my diet and stopped drinking alcohol. I am now happier and more confident than I have ever been in my entire adult life. And you can be too.

Humans are ready to evolve and raise their vibration. Evolving means uniting the mind, body and spirit. We can only do this by removing anything of a low vibration. This requires eliminating that which affects the smooth running of our brain and body. Only then do we see amazing changes in our life!

Wheat is Highly Addictive

I totally understand why the majority do not want to give up wheat. Most don't realize just how addicted they are to the grain or that they are not 'choosing' to consume wheat at every meal, an addiction is. Anything addictive puts up a fight to stay in the system. Our emotional attachments to certain foods are often stronger than our taste preference.

> 'Our decisions towards food choices are often not based on scientific findings but mostly on emotions and food attachments which are hard for people to break!'
>
> Dr Joel Fuhrman M.D.

When you remove wheat from your diet, you can then understand just how much it controlled your moods, appetite and mind. It also allows you to see other changes that need to be made. It's as if it unblocks the intuition. Your body may take a while to heal from a lifetime's consumption of wheat. But the good news is your mind heals very quickly and your Sensitive traits are easier to recognize and get back in control of. Eliminating wheat also allows us to get back in touch with our true hunger. We then eat when we are hungry as opposed to eating from false hunger or addiction.

If you do it, make sure you eliminate wheat 100%. Reducing your intake by 75% or even 80% will not see the changes you want. You may feel better for a while, but the addiction remains, meaning your consumption will creep back up until you are eating the same amount you were, if not more. This reinforces the addiction. The mind then does anything to stop you from giving up wheat again.

Eliminate wheat 100% for just four weeks and see for yourself the amazing changes. By changing your diet and tuning into your body's needs, it allows your true Self to emerge. Foods that act like drugs cause all humans damage. To the Sensitive, who already have many imbalances, drug-like foods are utterly destructive.

Facts on Wheat:

- **Wheat Makes You Overeat**:

  Consuming wheat encourages you to eat **at least** 400 extra calories a day. This has been scientifically proven!

- **Wheat is Addictive**

  It has an opiate-like effect on the brain, resulting in addiction and binge-eating.

- **Eliminating Wheat Can Make You Happy, Healthy and Slim**

Once wheat is out of your system you will not miss, nor crave it. Your moods will lift and you will enjoy vastly improved health.

- **Wheat Removal Makes You Look and Feel Younger**:

  Many people who have stopped eating wheat say they feel and look ten years younger.

- **Wheat Has Been Genetically Mutated and Hybridized:**

  The wheat we eat today is not what Mother Nature created. Its structure has been altered to such a degree that it is having a destructive effect on our health.

You May Eat Wheat at Every Meal

If you are under the impression that you do not eat much wheat, you may be surprised to hear, wheat is hidden everywhere. The majority of processed foods have wheat hidden within them, and not just in the unhealthy stuff. Crisps and snacks, frozen chips and vegetables, stock cubes, sauces and condiments, cheeses, soups, vegetarian products and nearly all ready meals (diet or not) contain wheat. Unless you are a stickler for reading labels, chances are you would not be aware of it. The good news is, there are many products out there that don't include the toxic grain.

It Would Not Be Allowed

You may now be pondering why wheat would be included in many of our foods if it was so bad for our health. If you consider there was once a time when smoking was considered healthy and prescribed by doctors, it may help you understand. Not everyone is aware of the danger wheat poses to the human body, although this is quickly changing. Wheat keeps us addicted, hungry and needing to consume more. Meaning, we keep buying wheat-containing products. As well as being a staple in the Western diet, wheat crops are a multi-billion-pound food industry. So, it should come as no surprise that the truth of how problematic wheat is, to health and wellbeing, is suppressed.

The Science Bit

Here, we will look at how wheat has evolved into the toxic grain it is today. Why it affects our mood and behavior and how it makes us overeat, overweight, and why it is best to be avoided by those who are Sensitive:

The first cultivation of wheat can be traced back to Southeast Turkey in 9000 BCE. It has been a staple in the Western diet for thousands of years. Globally, it is the third most produced grain after maize and rice. The world trade for wheat is greater than all other cereals combined.

The wheat we consume today is the product of genetic manipulation. The changes to its genetic code were introduced more than forty years ago.

How Wheat was Genetically Hybridized

Between the 1940s and 1960s there was a Green Revolution in which the world's agricultural production was vastly increased by the breeding and development of high yielding cereal grains such as maize, rice and wheat. It was intended and credited with saving over a billion people from starvation.

The changes to wheat began as far back as 1935 when genes for semi-dwarf wheat (Norin 10) were first bred by the Japanese Wheat Breeders. Dwarfing the wheat genes enabled greater seed production, and as it grew to just two-foot-tall instead of the usual four-foot, it was less prone to wind damage. This was then further developed by Norman Borlaug, known as the father of the Green Revolution.

Through genetic crossbreeding, Borlaug developed disease-resistant varieties of semi-dwarf, high-yield wheat.

By the 1970s, this semi-dwarf wheat was already being successfully farmed in Mexico, India and Pakistan. By 1985 much of the Western world was producing semi-dwarf wheat and by 1997, 81% of the developing world had introduced this crop. Interestingly, around the time this semi-dwarf wheat was introduced also coincides with the rise in obesity and diabetes epidemics.

Although the genetic crossbreeding of wheat was done to give greater yield, and thus end world famine, it also changed components of the wheat protein (lectins) known as gliadin. All it took was altering a few elements of the amino acids to change modern wheat into the appetite booster, health destructor and brain destroyer it is today.

Gliadin the Toxic Protein

Through scientific research it has been discovered that gliadin, in wheat, has created many of the problems within the human body.

To try to explain this as un-technically as possible:

19

Gliadin is a lectin and a part of wheatgerm and gluten. Lectins are proteins found within plants and animals that do the job of what antibodies do inside the human body: fight off foreign invaders like bacteria. Within plants, lectins ward off mold, fungi and other predators.

Lectins are found in many foods, yet the highest levels are in grains. Wheat has an exclusive form of lectin known as wheatgerm.

Stomach acid has little effect on lectins, they are virtually indigestible. When we eat food containing wheat, the lectins move undigested into the intestine. Our intestinal tract acts like a filter. It knows how to extract nourishment and remove waste from the food that passes through. Lectins disturb the intestines' natural ability to act as a filter which allows toxins into the body that cause damage and disease. These toxins, which have leaked into the body, wreak havoc on our physical systems and show up in many ways, such as: inflammation of the gut, bowel disease, arthritis, dermatitis, acid reflux, asthma, eczema, inflammation of the organs, imbalance in the endocrine system (glands which release hormones) and weight-gain/loss. But that is just the tip of the iceberg.

For those who are Sensitive these toxins also affect their sensitivities, heightening the more negative aspects of their traits and toning down the more positive.

Most people assume that you have to have a gluten intolerance to suffer wheat related illnesses, this is false.

Gluten is primarily found in wheat, rye and barley. So, those with gluten intolerance would need to avoid all of those. However, you do not have to be gluten sensitive to suffer the same debilitating ailments linked to it. All

20

you have to do is consume wheat.

Not only is gliadin bad news for the body, it also wreaks havoc on the mind and has an opiate-like effect on the brain which makes it addictive... this is the reason many do not want to give up wheat!

Wheat consumption is strongly linked to the plague of depression that has swept the planet. Depression is everywhere. Those who are Sensitive are often vulnerable to the condition and most have experienced it at some point.

In the 1950s it was estimated that no more than a 100 people out of a million had the need for antidepressants. That figure now stands at 1 in 10. More than 40 million people worldwide are on antidepressants.

According to the National Center for Health Statistics, in America alone the use of antidepressants increased by 400% between the years 1988 and 1994 and has continued to escalate.

Drug Inducing Effects of Wheat

Dr Christine Zioudrou, at the National Institute for Health, recognized a disturbing pattern between wheat consumption and mental health. She saw it had been observed, globally, by those treating people with Schizophrenia, that when their patients were exposed to foods made from wheat, they had hallucinations and heard voices. When wheat was taken out of their diets, the hallucinations stopped.

Dr Zioudrou questioned what it was in wheat that created Schizophrenics to react the way they did. In her bid to find out, she took wheat proteins and put them through the process of digestion. She discovered that when wheat was broken down, during the digestive process, it did so into many small proteins. These small proteins, called exoporphins, had the ability to cross the blood-brain barrier (a normally impermeable sheath that covers the brain) and bind themselves to the opiate receptors. This created negative behavioral changes and had the same effect of narcotics but without the high.

Another interesting discovery Dr Zioudrou made was that not only did the gliadin negatively affect mental health it also increased the appetite.

Tests were initially done on mice and then on a group of human volunteers. During the tests, the volunteers were injected with the drug Naloxone (an opiate blocking drug given to high heroin addicts to automatically reverse the effects) and were instructed to eat wheat-foods. When they ate wheat, after having the drug administered, they consumed about 700 calories. When the same experiment was done without the injection of Naloxone, they found the volunteers consumed at least 400 calories more! Proving the gliadin in wheat not only changes our personality and behavior, it also increases our appetite...

The Blood Sugar Connection

The Glycemic Index (GI) is a measure of how quickly the body metabolizes different carbohydrates. The higher the GI of a food, the more rapidly it is broken down and the faster it will spike blood sugar and insulin levels.

It is common knowledge that white sugar raises our blood sugars rapidly, but did you know that two slices of wholegrain bread raise it higher and faster than refined table sugar?

Wheat is 70% complex carbohydrate. Complex

carbohydrates are supposed to slowly break down into simple sugars when digested, which in turn leads to a slow release of sustainable energy. However, this is not the case with bread. Through glycemic testing, it was found that wholegrain bread is rapidly broken down into sugars after consumption. In fact, this breakdown starts whilst the bread is still in the mouth. This rapid breakdown leads to a huge surging sugar rush into the bloodstream.

High blood sugar is incredibly toxic to the cells of the body. If blood sugar levels rise too high and stay there, you will die. Therefore, to protect itself, the body has to find somewhere to safely put the sugar. The pancreas (producer of the hormone insulin) noting that the blood sugar is high, elevates the insulin levels.

Insulin is one of the primary hormones that stores fat and is known as the fat-producing hormone.

There are insulin receptors on the liver, muscles and fat cells. The first-place insulin is deposited is in the liver and muscles for short-term energy use. When these stores are full, the insulin receptors take the excess sugar out of the bloodstream and, with nowhere else to safely put it, transports the sugar to the fat cells, which turns to body fat and thus weight-gain!

If you do a lot of exercise or are naturally busy and energetic throughout the day, you may burn off much of the excess sugar stored from eating wheat and other refined carbs. However, the older you get, the harder this becomes and because the pancreas is constantly overworked, the excess blood sugar gets turned into dangerous visceral fat.

Look around at how many people over the age of thirty-five (and getting younger) have developed a bulge surrounding their midriff. (Especially obvious in those who are Sensitive.) Even the slimmest people can have a potbelly. For most, they are unaware that the protruding stomach, that will not shift even after diets and endless sit-ups, has been born from having repetitive blood sugar spikes following a lifelong consumption of wheat and sugar (combined with the stress that goes with it).

Sensitive people are vulnerable to having visceral fat (inner-fat) because their bodies often produce too much cortisol and adrenaline from having heightened emotions. Visceral fat is body fat that is stored within the abdominal cavity hidden, often between the organs, and is considered to be much worse than external body fat. So, we are at risk of having inner and outer body fat.

How and why does this happen? When cortisol and adrenaline are released into the body it stimulates the production of glucose (sugar). When it is not used, the body protects itself by turning the glucose into fat (fat is stored energy). For example: When gripped by negative emotions, as Sensitive people often are, the body is tricked into believing there is danger. It releases cortisol and adrenaline to turn into glucose for a quick rush of energy (to run away from this danger). But this energy is not needed. There is no dangerous threat, just strong emotions that have been triggered by a stressful event. The body has been put on high alert for no reason. The glucose (triggered by cortisol/adrenaline) is not used and instead is turned into fat, either internally or externally, which often ends up on the belly (Meditation and yoga help greatly with these stress responses. See chapters 7 and 8.)

As you can see, Sensitive people already produce too much glucose from having heightened emotions, the last thing we need is to have even more glucose dumped into the bloodstream by eating wheat (or sugar).

High Blood Sugar Leads to Diabetes

Diabetes has been on the increase around the world since the mid-eighties, which also coincides with the introduction of the new strain of wheat.

Diabetes is a disease where the pancreas ceases to work properly and stops producing insulin effectively. However, you do not have to have diabetes for your pancreas to breakdown. By consuming lots of wheat, the pancreas malfunctions to such a degree that the bloodstream has permanently elevated levels of insulin. When you have high levels of insulin, it promotes fat storage and prevents already stored fat from being broken down.

Obesity and diabetes are often blamed on the amount of refined sugar in the diet, which I am not disputing as being a huge problem, but as previously noted, wholegrain bread is worse than refined sugar for increasing insulin levels.

Wheat: A Dangerous Drug

There are some who may be surprised to read they are addicted to wheat. Yet, for most, it will make sense, even come as an 'aha' moment.

Just like refined sugar, wheat creates a dependence and addiction and like any other addictive substance, damages the body and the mind. To recover from any addiction and the harm it has caused, the addictive substance has to be removed completely. An alcoholic may be able to cut down his consumption of alcohol units, for a while, but it always creeps back up. With addictions there is no such thing as cutting down; the cause has to be eliminated. Alcoholics will always be addicted to alcohol as humans will always be addicted to wheat. Total elimination is the only answer.

It is simply the thought of giving up wheat which may fill you with dread, but don't let that fear stop you. Anything that has an opiate-like effect on the brain becomes addictive and alters perception. A wheat addiction prevents you from making rational choices. It saps your energy and clouds your judgment. Wheat has a strong emotional hold but, unlike refined sugar, the grain is hardly ever questioned or mentioned as one of the "dietary bad-guys" other than in food intolerances.

Mind-Altering Food

Wheat has the power to alter your perception and natural instincts; not only affecting how much you eat, but what you eat. Wheat is controlling you more than you could ever realize and not just in your dietary choices. It may play a part in other addictive behaviors and is strongly linked to controlling moods.

Until you take wheat out of your diet completely, then and only then will you see how it ruled your mind, moods and weight.

Everything Happens for a Reason

This book would not have come about had I not suffered most of my life with heightened Sensitivities, ongoing health issues, yo-yoing weight problems and debilitating chronic fatigue, which at times got so bad that even the smallest amount of movement left me with no energy. If I had not struggled with my Empath traits, had I been effortlessly slim, healthy and energetic, my fascination with health, exercise and diet would not have been born. And had it not been for an inner-suspicion that wheat was doing me no good, I may have passed Dr William Davies's claims off, that eliminating wheat would lead to weight-loss, as just another diet scam.

If as a Sensitive you are ingesting foods that your body sees as toxic, no amount of protection, holistic work, healthy eating, exercise or meditating will heal you, make you happy or get excess weight off.

There are many who look and feel good most of the time and include wheat in their diet, but those numbers are getting less and less. And just because one does not feel the ill effects of wheat now, does not mean they won't suffer in the future.

You will have reservations about eliminating wheat 100%. But please believe me when I shout:

'You will not miss wheat when it is out of your system!'

And that means freshly baked-bread, biscuits, cakes, croissants, pastries, pizzas or pasta (there are lots of incredible alternatives that taste just as good). You will not only look and feel great, but you can get back in control of your life, not to mention the weight-loss.

We all want to feel and look great and achieve a state of inner-bliss. And it is possible. Wheat elimination is the first step towards making these great changes happen. The next is sugar removal...

3

Oh Sugar!

I probably don't need to remind you that white sugar has no nutritional value, it is a toxic sweetener linked with diabetes, premature aging, obesity and many other diseases. Having a similar effect on the brain as wheat, white sugar acts as an opiate and triggers or worsens many health problems.

Refined sugar has been scientifically proven to be eight times as addictive as cocaine. This means sugar doesn't just act like a drug, it is a drug! Sugar is different from calories that come from food such as vegetables, natural fats and proteins. It jumbles our appetite controls and stimulates the urge to eat, even when we're not physically hungry.

Brain imaging studies done on humans found that eating sugar-rich processed foods lights up the brain like heroin. This explains why it is so addictive. If we regularly consume refined sugar, our dopamine receptors are downgraded, meaning we crave more and more of the sweet white granules.

Dopamine is a neurotransmitter that controls the reward and pleasure-forming centers of the brain. The more we indulge in addictive substances, the more we need of them to experience the same level of pleasure. And this is why it becomes such a challenge to give up sugar (and wheat). We are addicted to the dopamine release. Social media is known to produce large amounts of dopamine (hence the reason so many people continuously check their Facebook or Twitter accounts), but modern diets are mostly responsible for the problems with dopamine addictions.

Diet has more impact on the negative aspects of being Sensitive than you could probably imagine. When we have too many dopamine hits it reduces the production of serotonin, which is a bad thing. Serotonin is known as the happy hormone and is very important for the Sensitive (and every other human). Not only does it lift our moods and make us happy, serotonin is also a precursor for the body to produce melatonin, which helps regulate our sleep and in turn keeps us happy and healthy.

The problem we face is that we confuse pleasure with happiness. Pleasure is addictive. Happiness is not. There is no such thing as becoming addicted to happiness. People often mistake pleasure for joy. The irony is, the more pleasure we feel the less happy we become. The more dopamine the body produces the less serotonin (happy hormone) we produce. Anything that provides an artificial high, creates huge emotional lows. When the pleasure-forming centers of the brain are unnaturally stimulated, negative emotions later become aroused that can last for hours or even days after they have been triggered. In those who are Sensitive this negative response is felt as fear, anger, depression or some other type of emotional upset. These emotions, that have been artificially stimulated, create a ripple effect throughout the entire body. Not only do they weaken the gut and digestive system, but eventually work their way out to other areas and systems in the body, and greatly compromise all over health and wellbeing.

Most have not linked their heightened emotions to their consumption of refined sugar (or modern wheat). They take it for granted that this is how it feels to be Sensitive. But being Sensitive does not have to mean being in a constant state of emotional arousal. We can learn to control our emotions and traits but not when we are consuming drug-like foods that constantly activate them.

Removing refined sugar, and drug-like foods, from your life has a calming influence. Any heightened or erratic emotions are soothed, and you can learn to step away from the emotional roller-coaster. I would not have believed this had I not witnessed such a transformation within myself.

The Purpose of Food

We have to remember the sole purpose of food is to provide our bodies with nourishment and fuel to stay alive. As refined sugar has no nutrients, it has no benefit being included in our diet. Refined sugar is worse for the body and mind than cocaine, and more addictive, yet it is in most processed foods. Just like with wheat, when you've kicked the habit and got sugar out of the system, the addiction is gone for good. Have a small amount of it, however, and you will be back where you started.

Refined sugar is inflammatory. Inflammation is the root of all illness. If you have any health problems, consuming sugar will make them worse. And just because your body

30

looks healthy does not mean there are no underlying problems within. Many people experience niggling complaints (back pain, allergies, indigestion, low energy, etc.) that they don't realize are being caused by eating inflammatory foods. Removing sugar from your diet acts as a safeguard against unnecessary illness.

Wheat and refined sugars also rob the body of essential nutrients and enzymes. An imbalance of just one nutrient or enzyme can trigger illness and depression, it can cause chronic fatigue and sleepless nights and many other health problems. Generally, nutritional imbalances lead to a low-quality of life. Without enzymes we would cease to exist. They keep us alive, and nourish the body and mind. As we age, our enzyme production decreases, this, coupled with a bad diet, puts us on a fast-tracked-path to mental and physical illness.

As a Sensitive person, it is important to keep our enzyme consumption high and eliminate foods, such as wheat and sugar, that strip them, for the sake of our emotional health and happiness. Enzymes are found in all fruits and vegetables; but are especially abundant when the food is in its raw state, they can also be purchased in supplement form.

Time to Let Go

Giving up much loved foods, such as wheat and sugar, may not seem like a simple task. I know. Your cravings will fight with your mind to keep them in your diet. However, once out of the system, those cravings subside and you won't miss them. For anyone who has suffered a lifelong battle with ailments, allergies, fatigue and illness, you will be astounded just how much these foods affected you.

The Most Toxic Indulgences for the Sensitive

Sensitive people will not do well on any wheat or sugary foods. Until they are cleared from your system, you will not excel in life. I write this from experience.

Am I saying remove all sugars and sugar-forming foods from the diet? No, just toxic refined sugar and wheat. We need the good carbs like fresh fruits and veg (which also break down into sugars in the body) for our essential nutrients and energy. They are our superfoods and what nature intended us to eat. Even unrefined sugar once started off as a superfood before the refining process.

Unrefined sugar, or sugar beet, is packed with essential nutrients. Ever heard of molasses? This is the by-product of sugar refinement and is packed with essential nutrients, especially iron and the B vitamins. It is used to treat many health problems and is a popular supplement with a prominent nutritional profile. Because molasses or dark unrefined sugar retain their nutrients, they are good to use in cooking. They may take some time to get used to, as they can have a slight treacly taste, but when used sparingly and combined with protein or fat, won't spike your blood sugars or create addiction.

Other options, for sweetening food and drinks, are organic honey or maple syrup. For baking, unsweetened pureed dried fruit, like dates or prunes, makes an excellent sugar replacement. I also use small amounts of stevia or xylitol.

The Message

Not to want to be overly repetitive but it is crucial to get this message across: we do not miss sugar (or wheat) when out of the system and the withdrawal period has passed. I cannot convey just how important it is for your health and wellbeing. You will never regret eliminating them.

We do not need refined sugar in the diet. It provides no health benefits and only serves in making us emotionally unstable and eventually causes disease. Also, another point I would like to make at this time is how important it is, in our bid to clean up the diet, to avoid artificial sweeteners.

Artificial Sweeteners

There are no two ways about it, artificial sweeteners are toxic to the body. The words sugar-free on a label does not always mean healthy. It normally means it includes artificial sweeteners; especially in processed foods! Not only are they dangerous to our health, they are worse than the sugar they are imitating. They have been proven to make people crave carbohydrates and thus overeat. The majority who include artificial sweeteners in their diets for long periods of time will be overweight. That is why those who continuously slurp on diet sodas have little luck in losing weight or keeping it off. Artificial sweeteners are thousands of times sweeter than refined sugar and are linked to at least 92 health-related illnesses, from behavioral problems to brain-tumors. They stimulate our preference for sweetness and trick the body into believing sugar is on its way, which signals the pancreas to produce the fat-storing hormone: insulin.

These sweeteners are not a good substitute for refined sugar. In fact, they increase cravings and can be equally as addictive. Just because you do not sweeten your coffee or tea with them does not mean you are not including high amounts of artificial sweeteners in your diet. Like wheat, they are hidden in many places from drinks, foods, vitamin supplements (especially vitamin C and multi-vitamin drinks), gums and even baby food.

Read labels and avoid artificial sweeteners wherever possible.

The Elimination Process

Any kind of drug or stimulant only serves in weakening the Sensitive person; as they do any other human. Caffeine and alcohol also act like drugs. But we know they are drugs and very quickly see their effects after consumption. We will take a closer look at this subject shortly.

When you are free from the wheat/sugar addiction, you see exactly how they altered your moods, happiness and energy signature. You also become aware of any other changes you might need to make. You can see how other drug-like foods and drinks affect your 'Sensitive traits', and the idea of giving up other stimulants, such as alcohol or caffeine, doesn't faze you, because you've eliminated two of the most addictive substances known to man. Once you've given up wheat and sugar you understand that anything is possible! You willingly make changes, not because you feel forced into it, but because you want to.

Getting clean is not an overnight process, you often have to walk in small steps, but once you've had a taste of the emotional freedom that comes from being off the drug-like foods, you don't want to lose it.

Now, let's take a look at how the Sensitive brain affects our desire to consume drug-like foods, and how by their removal our life gets better.

4

Pleasure or Pain

One of the strongest driving-forces, for all humans, is the desire to feel pleasure and avoid all pain. Nearly everyone will go out of their way to stay away from anything that creates emotional or physical discomfort. But we are also strongly drawn to anything that gives great pleasure.

The most common form of pain, experienced on a daily basis, is emotional. This pain is caused by how we perceive our world. Speculative worries of the future, fear of being judged, fear of failure, or fear of not being liked, all lead to emotional pain.   Embarrassment, mortification and the many feelings that go with the perception of failure, cause untold misery. It is the type of 'pain' we go out of our way to avoid. We may try to hide from it, but by avoiding emotional discomfort it only makes our world smaller. Our opportunities for life experiences and growth then become greatly reduced.

We all want to stay clear of the pain caused by fear. Yet, as we live in a world that breeds it, it is nigh on impossible to do. For this reason, we cope by seeking out as many forms of pleasure as we can: food, drugs and alcohol being just a few. But what most don't take into consideration is that anything that comes with a false-induced high, also comes with a crashing low.

Those who are Sensitive gravitate towards emotional pain. Not by choice I might add, but by the law of attraction. Like attracts like. When we carry a lot of emotional pain (whether it is ours or not), we draw more of it to us. Feeling the sorrows of others, which become our own if we're not careful, only adds to our load. When a Sensitive person is psychologically low, they attract/sense this in those around them. There is so much anger, hurt and frustration in people these days that it is difficult to avoid. The public may disguise their angsts and insecurities behind pleasantries and smiles, but the Sensitive still pick them up, without trying. Spending time in the world can become like crossing a minefield. And this is why many Sensitive folk stay hidden away in their private sanctuaries, trying to avoid the explosive magnitude of human emotional pain.

In a bid to numb emotional pain, the Sensitive often overindulges in anything which gives the most pleasure or instant respite, as a way to try and block out what they feel. They unwittingly get addicted to wheat and sugary foods (and other forms of drugs) because they give a quick release of pleasure. But this relief is only temporary and comes with an almighty emotional hangover.

The short-term pleasure that drugs, alcohol or drug-like foods offer, activates more fear and more emotional pain. We then need to have more of the addictive substances. It becomes a vicious cycle. If consumed regularly, drug-like foods not only amplify all inner-fears and unpleasant feelings, but can eventually cause an unbalanced mind and emotional state.

The Sensitive Brain

It is known that parts of the brain that process emotional responses are hyper-reactive in those who are Sensitive. Because our brain sensors have been in a heightened state for most of our lives, they are overly affected by any negative stimuli we experience. Any upsetting event we experienced in the past has contributed to an inability to handle negativity in the present. Our responses to negativity and emotional pain are then worsened by drug-like foods or stimulants.

It is not just the Sensitive who react towards negative situations, all humans are hard-wired into focusing more on the negative than the positive. Because of the brain's negativity bias. However, any kind of unpleasantness affects the Sensitive person more than most. Because we are already vulnerable to negative emotional reactions, when around disagreeable people, it is important we remove anything from the diet that may add to these responses.

It has been found that the part of the brain which activates emotional pain is amplified in the Sensitive, and the part responsible for inciting happiness is less active. Those who have difficulty experiencing happiness often turn to alcohol, drugs, sweets and wheat as a quick pleasure-fix. Most are unaware that these stimulants contribute to keeping the natural happiness-forming part of the brain inactive. Therefore, pleasure can only be achieved by indulging in drugs or drug-like foods. But these reactions wear off quickly and are swiftly replaced by the low-level emotions of fear, anxiety or unhappiness. Hence the reason we go back for another fix. The part of the brain responsible for these highs and lows, is the amygdala.

The Overstimulated Amygdala

Dr. Elaine Aron, a research psychologist and self-proclaimed Highly Sensitive Person, has done much scientific research on the amygdala. In her studies, she found the amygdala to be overactive in Sensitive people when in circumstances that incite emotional responses.

Aron, who studied at the Jung institute and has a thriving psychotherapy practice, found through a series of trials and research, that when Sensitives were shown pictures of human suffering their amygdala became extremely active. She discovered this activation released excessive amounts of stress hormones into the body, such as cortisol and adrenaline. These hormones the further enticed more undesirable stress reactions, stoking fear and anxiety.

The amygdala is not a thinking part of the brain it is a reacting part. Meaning it activates when exposed to certain stimuli such as stress, fear, pain, and other strong emotions. It causes an automatic reaction known as the fight-or-flight response, which is the body's way of protecting us when we are in dangerous situations and need to flee. The process elevates the stress hormones, which in turn gives the body a rush of glucose, to give us energy to run away from danger or to stay and fight. However, the body cannot determine whether something is real or imaginary. Because the Sensitive person's dangers are mostly invisible threats (stemming from one's thoughts and emotions or the emotional energy of others), these hormones do not get used. For this reason, our body stays on high alert. The body should be activated like this only from time to time, but it can become a near permanent state in those who are Sensitive.

When the body is on high alert, it produces excessive amounts of cortisol. Which then leads to an excess of sugar (glucose) in the bloodstream. Signs you have too much cortisol in your body are: excess fat, especially around the belly area, feeling anxious or down, stomach problems, frequent headaches, a low immune system and extreme fatigue with an inability to sleep.

The Organ That Never Forgets

The amygdala retains all the negative and positive emotional memories one has ever experienced. These stored memories all have the potential to become trauma triggers or addictions.

If an experience or indulgence gives pleasurable feelings, the amygdala will urge us to seek out ways to experience it more often. If an experience was emotionally painful, the amygdala will react negatively towards any similar situations in the future. This can be said of incidents with people, pastimes or food. How our body reacts in the present, in regards to stress, anxiety, fear, anger or pleasure, is often determined by an event from the past. Even if we don't consciously remember a good or bad encounter, the amygdala does.

Addicts get hooked on drugs because the amygdala remembers the pleasurable experience the opiate and dopamine receptors triggered. It works the same when those who are Sensitive avoid certain negative people. The amygdala memorizes how it felt to be around them and issues a warning as a physical response. This is another reason why people become trauma triggers for anyone who is Sensitive.

Stress Response

To better explain the stress response, I will relate to experiments done on caged rats. It was found when the rats received painful shocks at the same time as specific sounds, they showed a stress response. However, at a later date, the same sound played without the shock would trigger a similar stress response. Although no shock was given, the rat was expecting to experience pain when it heard that specific sound. This was due to the amygdala's ability to link the memory of pain to the certain situation or sound. This type of reaction is also experienced by people.

If anything caused us a painful emotional response in the past, every time we are in a similar situation, we can experience this same reaction, yet have no understanding why. It also works the other way. If something gives us a sense of pleasure (such as foods that act like opiates), we can be drawn to the food purely by how it makes us feel.

The Addictive Amygdala

Most Sensitive people are known to have an addictive nature. This should come as no surprise when you consider the amygdala and addictions are connected.

It is understood by scientists, that the amygdala plays a huge part in addiction through its role in stimulating emotional responses, both positive and negative. When the brain stores a memory, it will also store the emotion that went with it. So, if a food activates the opiate receptors of the brain and creates good sensations, the memory of this food is then stored as being positive or pleasure-forming. Anytime we come across this food in the future, the amygdala remembers the pleasure it gave and urges the mind to eat it. If consumed regularly, the body then develops a craving. Wheat and sugar are the worst culprits for causing these cravings and thus addictions.

We remain mostly unaware of our addictions towards wheat and sugar because we don't crave them individually. Instead we hanker after the foods that contain them: pasta, cakes, muffins, breads, pizza, soda, sweets and candy. Addictions are habits which are difficult to break. Not only because anything that creates an addiction causes unpleasant withdrawal symptoms, but because our brain reminds us that these foods give pleasure and it's a pleasure it does not want to live without.

Anyone who has given up addictive substances, such as caffeine, alcohol, cigarettes, wheat or sugar, are only too familiar with the discomfort withdrawal can cause emotionally and physically. Because withdrawal is normally an unpleasant experience, it acts as a powerful motivator to resume an addiction. This is the reason many only manage to last a week or two in their bid to kick addictive habits. They don't realize that the discomfort and cravings would have soon passed.

How Painful & Pleasurable Memories Are Stored

The amygdala is the most involved brain structure in emotional responses and for creating emotional memories. The hippocampus transforms short-term memory into long-term memory and conveys emotional significance to stored memories. The amygdala and the hippocampus work together to create long-term memories of all the emotional events we have experienced. This dual activation is what gives emotionally based memories their individuality.

When emotions are aroused, the brain takes note and it stores as much detail as possible about the emotion-filled event, ready for quick recall. These memories can then be called upon at a second's notice, even after a long time has passed. The amygdala learns the level of danger or pleasure which should be linked to any particular trigger, but any negative responses can be heightened by consuming wheat and sugar.

Let me explain how these foods contribute to the storage of negatively charged memories: One day you have white toast and high-sugar jam for breakfast (wheat and sugar). Together they give an opiate-like high and a swift rush of energy. A few hours after breakfast you go to the shopping mall. By now the rush of wheat and sugar have worn off and you start to become grouchy or hangry (combination of hunger and anger). When you enter the mall, in this state of withdrawal, you automatically sense the emotions and energy coming at you from all the other shoppers. Because you are off-balance, you are also uncomfortable. You focus on this discomfort and start to feel emotionally overwhelmed. The amygdala is constantly taking note of these emotional reactions and stores the memory of where these crushing feelings took place... around people in the shopping mall. This emotional memory is filed ready for quick recall. To the amygdala, the mall is considered a threat or dangerous place to be. The next time you enter the shopping mall, the memory of the previous visit is recalled. As a warning the amygdala ignites the overwhelm, experienced on the last visit, as a reminder that this is not a safe location.

Sensitive people are known to react harshly to emotional triggers. If we continue to consume foods that heighten these reactions, the triggers and responses cause increasing levels of damage to the body and mind. Navigating emotions will always be a challenge for the Sensitive, and this is why it is important to remove anything that creates excessive emotional highs and lows.

Emotional dependence to foods such as wheat and sugar were normally developed in childhood. In particular at times of merriment. Parties and other celebrations are marked by the offerings of delicious cakes, sandwiches, pastries, chocolates and other indulgent foods, made from wheat and sugar. Happy memories of celebrations are then strongly linked to these 'treats'. We are powerfully drawn to certain foods and drinks because of the happy memories invoked within us. Even if they are hazardous to our health. Such is the pull of emotional memories.

The Part our Hormones Play

The endocrine system is responsible for releasing hormones into the body. It is a collection of glands that secrete more than 20 different hormones into the bloodstream. These hormones are like chemical messengers, each one having their own purpose.

You may not be familiar with the endocrine system but you will be familiar with some of the glands and the hormones they secrete: The pineal gland secretes melatonin and serotonin, the thyroid produces thyroxin, adrenals produce adrenaline, the pancreas releases insulin and the testes and ovaries secrete estrogen and testosterone.

Our endocrine glands react to specific stimuli and release hormones so the body can carry out a certain function. For example, in darkness the pineal gland will produce melatonin, known as the sleep hormone, which tells the body it is time to sleep. In times of fear the adrenals will ramp up production of adrenaline, which gives us the strength to run away from a dangerous situation, and when we consume starchy carbohydrates and sugars our pancreas releases insulin, which the body then uses to remove excess sugar from our bloodstream so it can be used for energy or be stored as fat.

Our chemical messengers have their own functions with the organs and tissues of the body, but they also work together. When one goes out-of-balance it has a knock-on-effect on the others. Wheat and sugar create a discord within the endocrine system because they quickly break down into sugar. This spikes blood sugar levels which in turn creates an overproduction of insulin. This not only acts as a catalyst for weight-gain but also offsets the other glands and the hormones they secrete.

The responses created by an imbalance in our hormones can cause an internal "drug-like addiction". When our blood sugar levels quickly spike, they also very quickly plummet. This fall then causes discomfort. To right this, the body/mind will produce a craving for a wheat or sugary fix. The body wants you to eat something that will lift you out of the slump and the quickest way for this to happen is by eating foods that elevate blood sugar levels: wheat and sugar! As soon as they are eaten, they induce feelings of calm and contentment. The mind and amygdala then associate these foods with pleasure.

As discussed in the last chapter, we start to rely on the highs that come from eating wheat and sugary foods, even though we are not always aware of it. Our mind has been tricked into believing we need them to give us pleasure and it is this pleasure-addiction that drives the desire and the reluctance to give wheat and sugar up.

Any type of addiction or artificially created high comes at a price to our health and mental wellbeing. The older we get, the higher the price we pay. From the mid-thirties onwards, we can see the destructive effects of our diet and lifestyle gnawing away at our happiness. Which only gets worse with each passing year. As Sensitives, we experience hormonal disruptions from our high-reactive nature and powerful emotions. We already produce too much of the stress hormones adrenaline and cortisol, the last thing we want is our diet to disrupt these hormones to produce even more.

The blood sugar roller-coaster and addictive urges towards wheat and sugar soon passes, once out of the body. It is not so much because of wheat and sugar's taste that drives us to consume them, it is the way the brain and chemical messengers react to them, making us believe they taste divine.

Will removing drug-like foods stop you being an Empath? No. Will it stop you being Sensitive or block other people's emotions? No. What it will do is make you healthier (if you follow the 4-week elimination plan), increase your happiness, and allows your emotions to become more balanced. Living in this chaotic world then becomes far more enjoyable. And once you've had a taste of this, you won't want to go back.

So, by now you should have a pretty good idea how wheat and sugar impact you as a Sensitive and indeed as a human. Just being told something is bad for us is often not enough, we need to understand how they affect us and why. Now we will take a look at how we can further soothe our emotions and build the brilliant life we were born to live!

5

Soothe the Seat of Emotions

The gut is the seat of our emotions and where we the experience the impact of all we feel emotionally. Sensations such as stress, hurt, anger, fear or other nervous tensions leave a direct impression on the gut leaving a trail of damage in their wake. Sensitive people are known to suffer with gut weakness and digestive health issues.

Nervous tensions activate the stress hormone cortisol. Cortisol is produced by the adrenal cortex. Like adrenaline, it is emitted in times of stress.

As part of the flight-or-fight response, the body produces extra cortisol which in turn pumps excess sugar into the bloodstream to provide sufficient energy to flee a dangerous situation or stay and fight. However, most Sensitive stress is actually triggered by invisible threats or emotional responses, but still generates the same hormonal release as danger. The excess blood sugar produced by this cortisol activation gets turned into belly fat which puts extra strain on the body.

Too much cortisol also causes carb cravings for wheat

and refined sugar. This in turn creates more emotional stress and more cravings. And the cycle repeats.

Coffee

Another thing that produces excess amounts of cortisol and triggers negative emotions is caffeine. Caffeine is one of the most over-used addictive substances available, especially in coffee. If you are sensitive to stress or other emotions, then too much caffeine can keep you in a hyper-stressed state.

The thing is with caffeine, most don't realize how it activates stress hormones, because it is the first thing reached for in the morning. As soon as we tumble out of bed, we enter the kitchen and the kettle goes on. Coffee (or tea) is then normally brewed. After drinking, it doesn't take long for the caffeine to get into the system. Caffeine stimulates the release of adrenalin and cortisol. These are what give that 'kick-start'. However, if you are sensitive to these hormones, it also triggers stress levels. Caffeine keeps the body in a state of high alert, expectant of impending danger, and switches on the sympathetic nervous system (SNS). Because those of us who are Sensitive already have an overworked SNS, the last thing we need is more stimulation.

You may notice the effect of caffeine by a tightening around your solar plexus (mid-stomach). If you drink too much it can trigger anxiety and panic attacks. I am not saying give up your favorite coffee entirely, just dial down consumption. You may be fooled into believing caffeine gives you energy, it actually does the opposite. Well, it might give you a kick-start at first. But what is given will be later taken back with interest. Caffeine stresses the adrenals. This action then weakens and overworks an already delicate body chemistry. If you drink coffee and become jittery or anxious, shortly after, or if you feel a tightness in your chest or stomach, your system has become too clean for that amount of caffeine.

A good way to quit the caffeine habit, is to mix half decaffeinated coffee with your favorite brew and gradually decrease the amount of caffeinated coffee over the week or weeks. You may not have to eliminate caffeine completely, but take note at which point your stress hormones are activated and keep it below that. Also, avoid drinking black coffee on an empty stomach.

Alcohol

Whilst we are on the subject of stimulants that trigger our emotions and the stress hormones, we should also take a look at alcohol. Many Empaths use alcohol to obstruct other people's energy, especially at social events. I can categorically state it does not work! Under the influence, it may feel like the emotions off others are being blocked, but this is not the case. Alcohol does not block people's emotional energy. If anything, it enhances its effect and leaves us filled with fear and ill-feelings for days after. How do I know? I drank for thirty years of my life. Now I no longer imbibe, I can see exactly what effect it had on my life!

Many, but not all, Sensitive folk are introvert in nature. Introverts dislike small talk, they need their conversations to have depth and meaning. They do not fare well in the social environments the rest of the extrovert world thrives on. Busy social settings are hard-work for the Empath, making them feel drained or overworked. Because the social traits of an introvert Empath are not seen as acceptable, in this extrovert world, many use alcohol to help them cope in social situations, hoping it will aid in more relaxed conversations. But, in the long term, alcohol does not make us happy. To be happy, we need to be authentic and true to ourselves. Alcohol prevents this from happening. If it is used to help in social events, we become dependent. We then believe we cannot have a good time without it.

When we become aware of being an Empath or HSP, we come to realize, when we drink alcohol, we often do so to handle being in certain people's presence for any length of time. We may also believe alcohol blocks out other people's emotions and numbs pain. It really doesn't!

When I was younger, I had fun times whilst drinking at parties. Back then I liked the social scene. But the more alcohol I drank the weaker and more fearful I became (although I had no idea of this at the time). The older I got, the more my introvert Empath traits kicked in, and the less I enjoyed the party lifestyle. After the age of thirty, my main reason for drinking, I thought, was to give me the ability to be around people comfortably. I assumed it lowered my 'negative energy sensors'. But alcohol just slowed down my reactions. I still had to deal with the energy I acquired off others, but I had to deal with it at the same time as a physical hangover. I did not understand, being an introvert Empath, I would not enjoy being around large groups of people. But no one had taught me this.

By giving up wheat, I could see how damaging alcohol was. I knew it was not making me happy... far from it. I listened to my intuition, which for too long I had ignored; telling me it was okay to give up. I had no idea how

51

fearful alcohol was making me or how much it held me back. Until I gave it up. I then experienced a contentment I had never felt in my adult life. This is because, like wheat and sugar, alcohol suppresses parts of the brain responsible for joy and happiness. People drink alcohol to have a good time but, the irony is, alcohol takes away the ability to have natural fun.

Drinking alcohol will not bring us peace of mind. It is not a release valve, and it does not help us relax after a long day at work. These are just illusions and what we tell ourselves to justify our drinking habits. Alcohol makes us ill, overweight, anxious and fearful. It heightens any negative emotions we have, whether our own or those picked up off others. Alcohol holds us back from taking risks or stepping from our comfort zone. If we reach for alcohol every time we feel uncomfortable, it blocks any chance for growth or self-development.

Like attracts like! If you are fearful and drink alcohol guess what you feel more of? Yes, more fear! Giving up the booze does not have to be difficult. It is as simple as deciding you want to transform your life and reach your true potential. You may have to give up your social life for a while. But it is worth it.

So, not only do caffeine and alcohol heighten negative emotions, they also hold us back in life and cause unnecessary nervous tension.

Nervous tensions produce acidity which lead to digestive health issues. Stomach problems are common with Sensitive people. Most doctors agree that there is a direct link between the emotional balance of a person and their susceptibility to gastrointestinal weaknesses and other illnesses. Another factor that causes weakness within the gut is 'Sensitivity stress'.

Sensitivity Stress

Sensitivity stress is endured by those who experience other people's pain or energy as an adverse reaction. They overreact to any emotional situation and are prone to having nervous tension. This type of stress is not caused by having deadlines to work to or a mammoth to-do-list (although they certainly won't help), it is caused by having a Sensitive nature, being overly stimulated from external energy and/or having buried emotional pain.

Even from a young age, Sensitive people frequently experience stomach aches, acid indigestion and bowel problems, produced by emotional upset. The sensations felt in the belly come from the enteric nervous system, a network of neurons lining our gut and responsible for butterflies and other emotional impressions.

With its ability to interpret certain emotive data, the gut is also known as the second brain. Science now recognizes that our emotions are directly influenced by our gut nerves, via the gut/brain connection. Everyone feels anger, fear and nervousness in the belly, but those who are Sensitive feel these emotions more intensely. So much so it can weaken the area. This means we are more vulnerable to experiencing disorders of the digestive tract.

It is important, when looking after our Sensitive health, to take measures to heal, soothe and nourish our gut. Whether we think we have problems in that area or not. The gut is integral to our entire nervous system. Those with poor gut health are known to suffer with nervous conditions such as anxiety, panic disorder, stress, an overactive mind and emotions. When we calm and heal the gut we calm and heal the brain, body and emotions.

There is a famous Hippocrates saying that '*All disease begins in the gut*!' I for one believe it to be true. Poor diet and stress, coupled with modern lifestyles, compromise gut health and causes inflammation or leaky gut.

For the Empath or HSP, having a leaky gut is our worst nightmare, especially when it comes to health and emotional wellbeing, and the last thing we would want to endure. Removing wheat and sugar goes a long way towards healing the gut and massively helps with the reduction of inflammation, but we can greatly speed up the curative process by including foods that nourish and heal the gut lining. The stronger and healthier the gut, the happier and healthier we are.

When it comes to gut healing, foods high in zinc and collagen, or collagen forming, are excellent. As are probiotics, prebiotic foods and L-Glutamine. All of which are available in supplement form.

Zinc: Zinc is used for treating depression and mental disorders, it builds the immune system and helps with wound and tissue healing. It is known as the anti-inflammatory, antioxidant and gastro-protective mineral, that aids with curing conditions of the digestive tract. Nearly everyone has some level of deficiency in this essential mineral and would benefit from supplementation as well as including an abundance of zinc rich produce into the diet.

Foods containing good amounts of zinc are: garlic, chickpeas, sesame seeds, dark chocolate, pumpkin seeds, salmon, shrimp, lima beans, egg yolks, turkey, spinach, kidney beans, mushrooms, flaxseeds and brown rice.

Collagen: Collagen is the most abundant protein in the body and the glue that holds us together. It is found within our skin, bones, tendons and muscles. As we age the production of collagen rapidly decreases.

Lower collagen levels lead to wrinkles and sagging skin, it also weakens our tissues and joints. Collagen is essential for gut healing, as it helps feed, repair and calm the mucous lining of the small intestine. If we want to increase our health and happiness, we need to keep our gut healthy. As well as removing collagen reducing foods, such as wheat and sugar, eating foods high in gelatin or vitamin C is the best way to get the body to produce more collagen.

The main function of vitamin C is to make collagen in the body. If there is no, or very little, vitamin C in the diet, collagen cannot be made.

Foods high in vitamin C are: lemons and citrus fruits, strawberries, kiwi, bell peppers, goji berries, Brussels sprouts, dark leafy greens, broccoli and black currants.

If you're not vegetarian and are open to eating animal protein, then one of the best ways to heal and soothe the gut is by eating bone broth.

Bone Broth: is touted as an elixir for gut health and is packed with gelatin, one of the greatest food sources for producing collagen.

Some consider bone broth to be the ultimate healing food as it is used to treat everything from infertility to Crohns disease. It is bursting with easy to assimilate minerals and all the amino acids the body needs. Good for the nervous system and the brain, it calms anxiety and balances the endocrine glands. Bone broth is most famously renowned for repairing disorders of the G.I. tract. It is a powerful curative food beneficial for all Sensitives (if they can get past the fact it is made from bones). See recipe on page 235.

L-Glutamine: This amino acid plays a huge part in healing and reducing inflammation in the gut. It also supports a strong immune system and helps reduce sugar and carbohydrate cravings.

Foods containing L-Glutamine are: Beef, soya, cabbage, spinach, parsley, eggs, cottage cheese, bone broth and asparagus.

Probiotics: Nutrient rich probiotic foods contain live bacteria and increase the colonization of friendly bacteria in the gut. Friendly bacteria line the gut and protect the digestive system as well as boosting the immune system.

Foods that contain probiotics are: live organic yogurt, sauerkraut, miso soup, kefir, sour pickles, and tempeh.

Prebiotics: While probiotics contain live bacteria, prebiotics feed the good bacteria already present and increase its colonization. Taken together they work powerfully to keep a happy, healthy gut.

You will find prebiotics in: prunes, bananas, oatmeal, Jerusalem artichokes, legumes, honey, maple syrup and garlic.

Garlic: The superfood which should be a staple in every Sensitive's diet is garlic.

Garlic is an amazing tool when it comes to healing the body; it is a powerful antibiotic, anti-fungal and anti-inflammatory, it helps remove heavy metals and contains potent antioxidants that build a strong immune system. Garlic has been used for thousands of years to treat disease of the mind and body and is known to protect and heal the digestive system.

Garlic speeds things up. It speeds up our vibration, both physically and energetically. It speeds up the metabolism helping shed excess weight, it speeds up the digestive system removing food and toxins and it speeds up the human energy field, meaning blocked energy or the energies picked up off others can bounce back off.

Another way garlic helps is in its anti-inflammatory properties. Stress caused by emotions, our own and others, can contribute to inflammation within the body. Inflammation causes disease.

Anyone who is highly Sensitive becomes stressed easily and need to take preventive measures to stop stress causing the body harm. By including garlic in the diet, it will go a long way to do this.

To get the full benefits of garlic you have to include it in your diet regularly. It is best to build up gradually. Too much garlic too soon can cause stomach upsets.

Some may find raw garlic to be problematic, causing an allergic reaction. If this is the case, you may find you are ok with capsules or garlic oil. You might be sensitive to garlic when eaten raw, but not when it is cooked. You have to play around with garlic dosage, sometimes less can be more.

Brain Food

As well as consuming foods that heal the gut, it is also advisable to include nutrients that protect the brain and nervous system. If we look after our brain it will look after us. Being Sensitive, having an overactive amygdala and eating a lifetime's worth of foodstuffs and chemicals damaging to the brain, it serves us no end to feed it with nutrients that are healing and empowering.

Having a strong nervous system helps us better deal with the Sensitive traits that create stress within the body. By choosing nutrients that support brain function it will not only protect us from neurological stress but from environmental toxins in the food, air and water, that are degenerative to the brain. The following have a strong neurological supportive profile and are incredibly beneficial to eat daily:

- **Omega-3 fatty acids**: oily fish, olive oil and egg yolks.
- **Vitamin D**: oily fish, mushrooms, peas, eggs, butter and cheese.
- **Turmeric**
- **Cold pressed organic coconut oil**

6

Nature's Elixir

When making changes to your diet, it is also a good time to increase your water consumption. Water is incredible for our health and when we are going through withdrawal, we need much more of it.

We could not survive more than a few days without water and this should make it clear how important water is.

Not only does an insufficient supply of water create problems with the functioning of the body and mind, it can also influence how we feel emotionally. Because Sensitive people are often on overload, from experiencing heightened emotions, our filtering systems don't always work as efficiently as they should, and toxins stay in the body longer than they should. And, due to the fact the body is fighting with an excess of toxins, its equilibrium becomes affected. We need a lot of water. Water helps flush out the toxins and helps keep us balanced and emotionally stable. This is especially important when removing wheat and sugar from the diet.

The body is comprised of seventy-five percent water (some body tissue has ninety-five percent), so it should come as no surprise that we need to drink lots of it to promote proper brain function, detoxify the body and stay healthy. When the body is out of balance through dehydration the brain is negatively impacted. Thoughts can become darker and one can become easily irritated.

Many are unaware just how dehydrated they are. An insufficient supply of water creates problems with the functioning of the body and mind. It also affects well-being and accelerates the aging process.

Breathing alone loses a quarter of the body's water on a daily basis. If you allow yourself to get dehydrated you are more prone to suffering anxiety and panic attacks and you may have low-level energy.

It can be difficult to know how much water we should be drinking. Every person's body is different, as is their water requirements, but aiming between six to eight pints a day is a good start (drank through the day, as opposed to the evening, so you're not kept up at night with bathroom visits).

A sign that you are not consuming enough water, can be seen externally as wrinkly or tissue-like skin, dry mouth, lips and eyes. Mild dehydration can cause headaches, dizziness, brain fog and fatigue. It may also lead to muscle weakness and a lack of stamina. Ongoing dehydration causes constipation, problems with the functioning of the kidneys and liver, and muscle and joint damage.

Dehydration also causes emotional stress, something Sensitive people already have too much of. Drinking plenty of water whilst enduring any type of stress, significantly reduces its negative effect on the body and mind. Water also helps diffuse and dilute negative energy picked up from others. It keeps the physical body strong and acts as a buffer to unpleasant energy.

Drinking water also helps ward off depression and low moods. Everyone should drink **at least** six large glasses of pure water each day to replenish what the body loses through sweating and urination. The heavier you are, and the more you sweat, the more water you should consume. As a general rule, if you are thirsty you are already dehydrated.

In a bid to stay hydrated, it is necessary to keep an eye on our mineral levels. When we consume high amounts of water, or sweat profusely, sodium and essential minerals are flushed from the body. When increasing water consumption, we should also increase our salt intake. But all salts are not created equal, at least not those bought in the supermarkets. The only mineral rich salt suitable for safe human consumption is either unrefined rock or sea salt and they must be organic.

Organic, unrefined salt is crystalline in structure and can easily be absorbed by the body. This is because the blood has a crystalline structure. Unrefined salt is packed with essential minerals vital for good health. My favorite is Himalayan crystal rock salt, which has the full spectrum of 84 trace minerals and elements (regular table salt has only 4). You can safely add this to your food, or allow a small particle to dissolve on the tongue, before slowly drinking a pint of clean fresh water.

When you increase your water intake, you quickly see an improvement in your physical and mental well-being. You also find your natural thirst develops, which ensures you stay adequately hydrated.

By drinking lots of lovely water, it helps flush out anything that doesn't get removed by the body being on 'high alert' – or on emotional overload – and thus aids in keeping the energy body strong. A strong energy body helps keep us protected from the emotional energy of others. It also helps keep the physical body strong, which in turn acts as a shield to any external unpleasantries.

Water not only feeds all the body's cells but acts as a buffer and cleanser of negativity.

Apart from staying well hydrated, one of the easiest ways to see water's powerful cleansing effect is to jump in the shower straight after coming home from work or after time spent in peopled places, and see the uplifting effect it has. For maximum energy-cleansing-benefits, make sure the crown of the head goes under the shower (which means getting the hair wet). If you're not a shower person, a bath works equally well.

Water really is an easy elixir for all Empaths and HSPs. We need lots of the stuff to help us stay healthy, happy and grounded.

Drinking water also helps ward off depression and low moods. F. Batmanghelidj, M.D., author of 'Your Body's Many Cries for Water', says in his book:

"Pathology that is seen to be associated with social stresses—fear, anxiety, insecurity, persistent emotional and matrimonial problems—and the establishment of depression are the results of water deficiency to the point that the water requirement of brain tissue is affected." He writes: "With dehydration, the level of energy generation in the brain is decreased. Many functions of the brain that depend on this type of energy become *inefficient. We recognize this inadequacy of function and call it depression."*

During stressful periods or times of change, such as starting a new exercise regime or changing your diet, it is even more important to keep your water levels high. Doing so will help keep you balanced and grounded and build a stronger defense against any overwhelm you may experience.

7

Fundamentals of Exercise

To have a healthy body and mind, not only should we look at changing our diet but also make sure we are exercising.

There is no getting away from the importance of exercise. It is essential for all humans and should be considered a staple in daily life for those who are Sensitive. If you want to stay healthy in mind, body and spirit, doing some form of exercise is a must.

Exercise is brilliant for dealing with pained or stressed emotions (especially anger), depression, our own or erratic energy picked up from others. But that's not all: Exercise works the heart, burns fat and keeps you strong, it also reduces stress hormones (produced from having heightened emotions) it also helps promote serotonin production.

Serotonin is a very important hormone for the Empath and HSPs. Not only does it lift our moods and make us happy, it is also a precursor for the body to produce melatonin, which helps regulate our sleep.

Anything that makes us happy attracts more reasons for us to be happy. So, if doing something as simple as working out for ten to twenty minutes a day can make that happen, there is no excuse not to do it.

If you have not exercised in a long time, work your way back into it gradually, but do something every day, no matter how little. Start with a short daily walk and some gentle stretches and keep adding a little more each day.

When it comes to exercise, we are all different. Some love physically demanding sports and some love to do more gentle exercise like yoga. From my research and self-trials, I have come to understand we need both. High intensity exercise works the heart, burns off negative emotions, produces human growth hormone and releases feel good endorphins. Yoga, or stretching exercises, keep the muscles strong, flexible and less injury prone. Yoga also helps negate the stress hormones and is incredible for the mind, body, spirit connection. Let's look a little closer at the types of exercise that will help do that:

High Intensity Interval Training/Exercise (HIIT):

Of all the high intensity exercises there are, HIIT seems to get the best results for releasing the right kind of hormones. HIIT may sound scary but it is simply working the body to its utmost capacity for a short duration of time, which is different for everyone. Low to moderate intensity intervals of exercise are alternated with high intensity intervals for as little as a ten-minute workout. Even though the workout time is short the results are incredible. It might sound unbelievable that we can work out for ten minutes and get better results than putting ourself through an hour's gym-slogging routine, but there is science backing it up and the results speak for themselves.

HIIT is one of the best ways to get the body to produce human growth hormone. A hugely important hormone when it comes to staying healthy and happy. Human growth hormone (HGH) is secreted by the pituitary gland in the brain and is crucial for growth and repair of the body's cells, and for strengthening the immune system. HGH rises in childhood, peaks in puberty and declines from the thirties onwards. It is known to be beneficial for autoimmune diseases, healing wounds and injuries, and for staying youthful. HGH can turn back the body's internal clock, helping us slash fat, build muscle and increase energy levels. HGH is also known to have a potent effect on mood disorders and promotes emotional stability. Basically, human growth hormone makes us feel great.

High intensity interval exercise (HIIT) activates the super-fast muscle fibers. They are the only muscle fibers to produce HGH. A study published in *Sports Medicine* found that just ten minutes HIIT exercise is enough to secrete human growth hormone.

HIIT can be applied to running or walking. For example: you could spend ten minutes on a treadmill, alternatively walking for one minute and then running for the next minute. Or, on a stationary bike, pedal as fast as you can, for fifty seconds, then slow right down for a minute, until you catch your breath, repeat again until your short allotment of time is up. As long as you put maximum effort into the short burst of exercise you are on the right track.

If you are in good health and are willing to build up your fitness levels, you are an excellent candidate for HIIT. If you are unfit, or have not exercised for a while, speak to your doctor or a qualified fitness instructor about the best ways to build up your body, ready for high intensity interval training.

If you go to YouTube and type in HIIT for beginners you will find many techniques that can be performed at home or the gym. Just make sure to warm-up your joints and muscles first, to prevent injury, and always listen to your body. Never exercise through pain. If you start to feel unwell stop.

So, we've looked at the higher impact exercise, let's look at the one known to be calming to the body and mind, and nourishing to the spirit:

Yoga

Not only is practicing yoga great for strengthening and stretching the muscles, it also soothes the body's energy centers, relaxes the nervous system and reorganizes neural circuits in the brain. Yoga is also incredible for stabilizing negative emotions.

When we feel fearful emotions, it triggers the same hormonal response as danger within the body, and an excess of cortisol or adrenaline is released. These are the hormones that can keep us in a state of fear or emotional pain. Because yoga works on harmonizing the smooth running of the endocrine system, the stress hormones are greatly reduced.

The endocrine system is part of the body's chemical messenger service which secretes hormones into the bloodstream as and when needed. Because Empaths experience an excess of unnecessary emotional stress, their endocrine systems get overworked. Yoga helps re-balance the endocrine glands and energy centers, basically making more of the happy hormones (serotonin) and less of the stress hormones (cortisol and adrenaline).

Which Style?

Depending on your type, depends on which type of yoga would suit you. My advice is to try different styles and choose the form that makes your heart sing. There is a style to suit everyone. There are even forms of yoga that work in a similar way to high intensity interval training, which are suitable for those who like high intensity workouts. Or, you could combine the styles.

I believe the best types of yoga, that help keep the mind de-stressed and body strong and flexible, are the styles that sync the postures with the breath, otherwise known as dynamic yoga.

I have been to many yoga classes where the focus is only on the posture, with hardly any attention to the breath, and the yoga didn't have the same blissful effect. When we combine breath with movement it becomes meditative. It also helps us recognize where we have physical or energetic blockages in the body (the breath tends to become labored when there is a blockage or weakness).

I have spent many years studying yoga. I believe in its power so much that I qualified as an Ashtanga yoga teacher. After years of avid practice and study on the postures and their benefits, I became aware of how difficult teaching yoga is. For the reason that every person is so different in their physical. What benefits one

68

person will not benefit another. Where one may feel physical discomfort in a posture, another will feel nothing, and what is healing for one is damaging for another. Yoga is much like everything else in life, we have to listen to our own body and do what is right for us. Just because one person achieved many benefits by doing a pose in a certain way, doesn't mean it is right for us. If performing a pose in a particular way is not suitable for our body type, we feel it. Even our yoga teacher may not always know what's best for our body. If a teacher has not had the same obstacles to overcome, they will not always relate to those who have. And if they have not experienced heightened emotions or high levels of stress hormones, they may not be aware of techniques that can soothe or balance them. I am in no way trying to be disrespectful to yoga teachers here. But if you are going to start a practice, it is important to listen to your own body (but any good yoga teacher will tell you that). This also helps in discovering which poses are most beneficial to practice.

When yoga postures are combined with the breath it is known as dynamic yoga. Ashtanga Vinyasa is one type of dynamic yoga (but there are many more). Ashtanga is a very strong practice but which can also be modified for beginners. If you are a complete novice to yoga, a lovely style to try is Dru yoga. Dru combines movements with flowing breath and visualizations. It is suitable for all levels and all ages. It is a style that can be learnt online (which cannot be said for some types) or in a class environment. It is popular in the UK and Ireland. Their website is www.druyoga.com, where you can find free tutorials as well as more in-depth information about the style, and where to find classes.

Pilates is another exercise technique that is beneficial. Pilates obviously isn't yoga but it is very similar in its structure and is a derivative thereof. It also combines breath with movements, whilst focusing on the core. If you have a weak back, Pilates is a good choice because it focuses heavily on the safety of the spine.

If you are inflexible, do not let that put you off attempting yoga. When I started practicing, I could not touch my knees in a forward bend, never mind my toes. But that soon changed.

Many men are put off trying yoga because of their inflexibility, but men tend to progress much faster than women. Amongst many other things, yoga is about building strength and flexibility. Men tend to need to work on flexibility, whereas women need to build more strength. Muscles become pliable much sooner than they become stronger, and this is why men tend to see results in their practice sooner than women.

Another reason some avoid yoga is because after a few attempts they don't like how their body feels during practice. But again, this soon changes. I didn't like yoga when I first started, but I kept going because I knew it would help me. My intuition told me sticking with yoga would be worth it, and it was. I still have days when I don't want to practice, but after the initial push to get me on the mat, I am so glad I put the effort in.

When learning yoga, it is best to do it under guidance. I know, only too well, that yoga classes are not the best environment for Empaths and HSPs (too many people in small spaces), but they are good for learning the basics of safety and alignment. After a few classes, you could then continue your practice at home. If you cannot face a class environment, there are some excellent online

70

tutorials that are a good starting point. All you need is a mat and a small space to practice. If you go to my blog (www.theknowing1@wordpress.com) and type yoga in the search bar you will find links to videos suitable for beginners.

8

Mind Control

There is a saying that if you have a happy mind you will have a happy life. It is such a simple but true statement. *'What consumes our mind controls our life!'*

When making changes to the diet it is also a good time to develop a meditation or 'thought quietening' practice. Here's why:

Stilling the mind and balancing the brain, are essential steps to take to stop the ravenous and often incapacitating thoughts many Empaths and HSPs endure. If we do not control our thoughts, we will struggle to re-balance the amygdala, insula, limbic system and our hormones. After all, negative thoughts trigger negative emotions and negative emotions trigger negative thoughts, all of which are the catalyst to producing stress hormones. Meditation and breathing techniques are the best way to get back in control of the mind and prevent the darker thoughts, that may have shaped our reality, from being activated.

Meditation is one of the most powerful tools we can use to gain mastery of the mind. A committed daily practice serves in many ways: It helps release serotonin (the happiness hormone), it strengthens the mind, body and spirit, and helps build a powerful shield against negative energies. It does this by reprogramming the brain into better coping with negativity. This helps us deal with other peoples' thoughts, energy and emotions. And, because it makes us more balanced and peaceful, it helps us better deal with any negativity we may encounter and that includes resistance to diet changes.

Although it may be a challenge to develop a practice, especially when one has a creative and overactive mind, it is a super-effective way to stay in control of negative thoughts. Perseverance is all that is needed. Dark thoughts are addictive and difficult to break free from. The problem is, we are often unaware when we are wrapped up within the negative thinking process, and because of this we don't realize how our thoughts are impacting our life. But, once the mind is reset, through meditation, we gain greater control of what thoughts we engage and those we don't.

Meditation gives results, fact!

There is a reason so many successful people swear by meditation for creating the life they want... because it works. If the mind has been influenced and consumed by painful situations and stress hormones for the majority of our life, it may be uncomfortable to get into a practice. But repetition and consistency are all it takes. Not only is a daily meditation practice essential to calming our thoughts, it also gives access to our higher self and intuition like nothing else. It is our higher self that knows our best interests. It holds the answers that our rational mind doesn't. Our intuition lets us know where we should be going in life and stops us going down unnecessary paths. Also, certain aspects of life, that may not have made sense, will all of a sudden have such clarity. We come to understand why we had to travel the path we have (even if at times it was unbearable).

It is amazing how great our understanding becomes, when the mind is quiet enough to hear the voice of our higher self and intuition. By developing a regular meditation practice the voice becomes more audible and reliable. It is in the quiet, we hear the answers we need. Being able to still the mind may take time and effort, but in doing so, we ignite our inner-power.

Meditating doesn't mean we never have thoughts again. We simply gain greater control over those we choose to focus on. This ultimately prevents us from getting lost in the type of thoughts that trigger painful emotions. Which is especially beneficial if we take on the thoughts and emotions of others, as well as having our own to deal with.

Most envisage meditation as sitting with their legs wrapped around the neck, or in some type of pretzel shape, but you will be pleased to know there are many types that don't involve sitting on the floor in the lotus position. We don't even have to sit down or stay indoors. We can do a walking meditation where we externalize our awareness and focus on everything around us. For example: when walking outdoors, focus attention on your feet as they gently move over the grass, or look up at the trees and observe the sunlight reflecting sparkles of light off the wet leaves, or notice the cloud formations in the sky above. When practiced with awareness, yoga is a moving meditation that unites body, mind and spirit, and is a good option for those who do not like to sit still. There is a type of meditation to suit everyone. Chanting, breath-work, visualization and trance, are all ways of stilling the mind. Try out a few techniques and see which works best for you.

It should also be noted here that falling asleep in meditation is not advisable. During meditation, it is the time to quieten a busy mind through our own intention. If we fall asleep, we lose that opportunity. There are some who will say it is perfectly acceptable to sleep if we are tired. But I would suggest have a snooze first, then meditate after.

When we first meditate, mind chatter often steps up a gear. It feels like the world and his wife has taken up residence in our head... all with very loud voices. This is the egoic mind at work, wanting to stay in control of the thought process. This is entirely normal, albeit somewhat frustrating. And, just like turbulence on a plane, when we push through, we eventually climb above it. Then, all becomes calm and serene, and we find ourself in a state of bliss.

As with anything in life, good things don't happen overnight. The more we practice the calmer our thoughts and emotions become, and the more incredible we feel. Most notice the remarkable effects of meditation some point after the two-week marker (providing meditation is practiced daily). We relax, the mind becomes clearer, we feel stronger and empowered, and our thoughts are less hectic.

Meditation is a must for gaining control of the mind, but it is also a great technique for balancing our energy centers, as well as being anti-ageing, de-stressing to the body and an incredible aid to deep healing sleep, especially when done in darkness.

Meditating in the dark helps keep the pineal gland (third eye) healthy, which in turn keeps the production of melatonin balanced. Melatonin is known as the anti-ageing hormone and is produced by the pineal gland in darkness. It is a naturally occurring hormone, which regulates the sleep cycle, that is both an antioxidant and anti-inflammatory and helps prevent, and treat, many illnesses including cancer. Those suffering with insomnia or with mild sleeping difficulties are thought to have a melatonin deficiency. The immune system does most of its work at night and is believed to be interlinked with the production of melatonin. When levels are suppressed, illness occurs. Also, as we age, melatonin production decreases. Scientists believe this reduction is interrelated to ageing and age-related disorders. You can produce more melatonin, simply by meditating in darkness. Which is further aided by focusing on the third-eye (center of forehead) during meditation, which in turn stimulates the pineal gland.

The best way to meditate, for better mind control, is with an erect spine; sitting in a straight-backed chair or in a comfy cross-legged or kneeling position on the floor. Keeping the spine straight and upright allows energy to flow up and down without interruption, and keeps the breath calm. But one magic ingredient for an incredible meditation practice is using breathwork.

Being a yogi, and qualified yoga instructor, I know the importance of using breathwork, not only to help quieten a busy stressed mind, but also for balancing masculine and feminine energy, for removing impurities and blocked emotions. In fact, controlling the breath is, I believe, one of the best ways to get into a blissful state of mind. It is also so simple to do. Starting your practice with awareness to breath is the fastest way to get you on the right track.

So, to begin a meditation practice, it is best to plan a set time every day. Early morning or before bed is best. Perhaps start with ten minutes and build to twenty or thirty over the weeks/months. Having no distractions is important. If you think someone will walk in and disturb you, that's all you'll think about when you're supposed to be meditating. If there is a lot of external noise, pop some earphones in and play some gentle music, or listen to a guided meditation... As long as you practice regularly, you will continue to see the many incredible benefits of meditation unfold. If you don't know where to start you can go on YouTube and try some meditation for beginners (If you go to my blog, www.theknowing1.wordpress.com and type in meditation, it will bring up some techniques that are suitable for beginners).

A brilliant breathing technique that can be used to start your practice is alternate nostril breathing (is also great to use at bedtime if you cannot sleep).

Technique: Sit in a comfortable position. Using your right hand, place your thumb on your right nostril and close it, inhale through your left nostril, cover your left nostril with your ring finger, lift the thumb and exhale through the right nostril, this is immediately followed by an inhale through the right, close the right nostril with the thumb and exhale through the left nostril. This was one round. Start by practicing for one minute and build up gradually. Remember, it is on the exhale that you swap the nostrils you breathe through.

If one of your nostrils are blocked, you can do this technique through visualization. With the eyes closed, visualize the breath coming up through the left nostril and out through the right, in through the right out through the left, and so on...

9

What to Expect During Elimination

Ok, so getting back to the eating plan. Let's look at what you can expect by adopting a healthier way of eating. One thing that brings many people over to a wheat and sugar-free lifestyle is the premise of losing weight and getting rid of a bulging belly for good. On this plan most lose weight effortlessly and keep it off; which may seem impossible to those who have spent their lives yo-yo dieting, but it's true. There is no need to count calories or burn them off through vigorous exercise, as long as the glycemic load of each meal or snack is kept low, excess weight will be lost.

The only ones who do not see weight-loss, when they go wheat and sugar-free (and in some cases put weight on), are those who replace wheat fare with store-purchased gluten-free breads, cakes and biscuits. These food replacements are counter-productive as they turn to glucose in the body faster than refined sugar.

It has to be noted that you only lose weight if you need to. I hear many people say that they do not want to give up wheat or sugar because they don't want to lose weight (although I believe this is often an excuse). But if you are not carrying excess weight, you will not lose it. You can, however, still reap all the other amazing health benefits of being wheat and sugar-free. That said, just because you do not have body fat on the outside does not mean you don't carry fat on the inside. It is being discovered that some slim people (even children) have dangerously high levels of internal fat, which poses more of a health risk than external body fat.

Addictions and Withdrawal

Anything that creates addiction normally has a withdrawal period when eliminated. Wheat and sugar both create dependence and act like drugs. On their removal, the body may kick up an almighty fuss but it soon passes. Withdrawal can last from a few days to a few weeks.

Unfortunately, on any path to transformation you often have to endure an unpleasant stage. Try to look at it as the darkest hour before the light. It is like a healing crisis. As the body starts to heal, it goes through a state of shock, the brain goes into detox as the chemical messengers start to reset (another reason drinking water is so important). But once though the other side, you see the benefits are more than worth it and any discomfort is soon forgotten. That said, not everyone undergoes any ailments. We are all different. But if you know what to look out for, you understand what is happening should the symptoms arise.

The good news is there are ways to help minimize these symptoms and make them more bearable, which we will look at shortly. For now, let's take a look at what you may experience:

Emotional Withdrawal Symptoms

- Anxiety or panic attacks
- Restlessness
- Irritability
- Insomnia
- Headaches
- Poor concentration
- Depression
- Social isolation

Physical Withdrawal Symptoms

- Sweating
- Racing heart
- Palpitations
- Muscle tension
- Tightness in the chest
- Constipation
- Tremors
- Nausea
- Flu-like symptoms
- Body weakness
- Dizziness
- Sleep disturbance

Heal and Deal with Withdrawal

Not everyone experiences any of the above symptoms. But most have to endure at least one or two. Withdrawal often feels like you are under the weather with particularly low energy levels. It can be a strange time. Your body usually feels cleaner inside, as you are not feeding it the 'drugs', but at the same time you may have debilitating symptoms that make you weary.

During the withdrawal period, your body needs nurturing. Here are some simple but effective ways to help get you through the discomfort withdrawal may bring:

Hydrate: Drinking good amounts of water helps the body detoxify and flush out impurities caused from withdrawal. (See chapter 6)

Depending on your body size will depend on how much water you need, but it is advisable to drink at least double of what you would normally (minimum eight to ten glasses of clean fresh water).

Include lots of herbal teas, especially ones that are good for boosting the immune system such as lemon and ginger or Echinacea and berries.

Salt: When drinking a lot of water, essential minerals can get flushed from the body. It is important to replace them with a good trace element salt such as Himalayan Rock Salt. Add to your meals or allow a small salt crystal to dissolve on the tongue before downing a pint of fresh water.

Magnesium Citrate: Taking magnesium supplements helps relax muscles, balance blood sugar, reduce anxiety and aids in a better night's sleep. It also helps bowel movements for anyone suffering constipation.

Most people are already deficient in the essential mineral, magnesium, and see positive results by regularly including it in their diet.

Rest: Sleep as much as your body needs. The body goes into shock when drugs are removed and will need more sleep and rest than normal.

Try not to do anything too physically demanding if feeling weak. Listen to your body's needs and do not feel guilty for taking time out to rest.

Nature: Taking gentle walks in nature is a great way to fill the lungs with fresh air, which oxygenates the blood and calms the mind. It is both relaxing and rejuvenating without being taxing on the system. (See chapter 14 for the incredible healing benefits of being in nature)

Being outdoors, in quiet places, is always beneficial to those who are Sensitive, whether they are going through withdrawal or not.

Sweat it Out: A perfect way to help the detox period is by having a good old sweat.

During the first couple of weeks after wheat and sugar elimination you may feel too tired to engage in any activity that produces sweat. Using a sauna or steam room is a perfect remedy for sweating the toxins out.

Eat Nutrient-Dense Foods: Let food be your medicine!

Including lots of nutritious, organic foods into your diet is a fantastic way to reduce or eliminate withdrawal discomfort. Look to include dark leafy and cruciferous vegetables, citrus fruits, garlic and any other bright colored fruit and veg, quality fats and proteins.

Aromatherapy Baths: Taking a relaxing bath, with a few drops of lavender, is a perfect way to unwind and de-stress. Essential oils work directly on both the limbic and nervous systems to heal, aid relaxation and help restore balance (See chapter 16).

The Benefits of Wheat and Sugar Elimination

The incredible benefits of being wheat and sugar free will keep on unfolding. Within weeks of their elimination, many people say they feel and look 10 years younger. A healthy glow returns to the skin and the sparkle back to the eye. The lust for wheat and sugar-filled foods, such as bread, cake, biscuits and pizza, disappears along with the mindless addiction. But be warned, any addiction can be very quickly reignited. Think of wheat or sugar like heroin. A recovered heroin addict cannot try even a little of the drug, once he has got clean, without getting hooked again.

It takes twenty-one days to clear an addictive substance/food from the body, although it may take slightly longer for the mental addiction to pass. Depending on their severity, the side-effects can take up to twelve weeks to subside.

Going wheat and sugar free is the most important step you will take for transforming your life and health.

Being Sensitive makes us vulnerable to emotionally induced illness. We have to care about our physical and mental health, and one of the first steps to do this is by removing drug-like foods from our life.

> *If after the elimination of wheat and sugar you feel only marginally better, but not amazingly well, there's a chance you may have a gluten intolerance, food sensitivity, leaky gut or autoimmune disorder. This is further explained in the next chapter.*

When we continue to consume mind-altering foods, the world is a much darker place to live. Life has so much to offer but if we live under a dark cloud, and carry a weary soul, we miss the best of it. I am speaking from experience. I now know exactly what food does to our mental health and our Sensitivities. I have seen what happens when we eat drug-like food or food that does not agree with our body chemistry. It is not good!

The diet really can make or break you, and be the biggest blessing or blight on your life. Any inner-emotional pain is magnified by consuming drug-like foods and foods you are intolerant to. But you will not know how the diet affects you until you remove wheat and sugar!

The anguish and overwhelm experienced by those who are Sensitive does not have to be debilitating. Change your diet, change your life. Gain an emotional freedom you never thought possible. You can do it easily and effortlessly! Once wheat and sugar are out of the system, then and only then can you see how destructive it has been to both your health and your Sensitivities. However, by making these changes you won't suddenly become an out-and-out extrovert who loves being in densely populated places, if you are naturally introvert. Your lovely quiet traits will still dominate, but you won't be unnecessarily taken down by the overwhelm that comes with being out-of-balance.

After elimination, you may notice many of your niggling ailments have cleared up since going wheat and sugar free. Conditions like indigestion, acid stomach, bloating, acne, mood swings, lethargy, psoriasis, dry-skin patches, flaky scalp, fatigue and IBS symptoms typically get better soon after elimination (takes longer for some than others). And your waistline should be evidentially shrinking.

What Will Happen if I Eat Wheat and Sugar Again?

Quick answer: Don't. Ever!

If you start eating wheat and sugar again, if only small amounts, you will see any benefits accrued quickly disappear, and you may find you suffer with raging emotions, hormone and chakra imbalances, brain fog, irritability and a huge people intolerance. Any weight you lost will return and more besides. The health problems, which cleared up, reoccur with a vengeance and probably some new ones you didn't have before, show up too.

Why?

Wheat and refined sugar are toxic to the body, when you eliminate them from your diet, your body cleans up and is happy. However, put them back on the menu and your body will retaliate big time! It will scream at you to get your notice. Wanting to alert you that these foods are poisoning, it does this the only way it can through emotional upheavals, depression, personality disorders, aches, pains, illness and skin eruptions.

How does this happen?

When the body is clean, it feels the effects of toxins immediately. Think of a dirty puddle and picture what would happen if you poured more muddy water into it... you would not see a difference. This is because you are adding muddy water into muddy water. Now, picture the puddle being crystal clear, what would happen if you poured muddy water into it...? You see the effects instantly and dramatically.

The above analogy can also be used with the diet: Put wheat and sugar into an unhealthy body, that has been having them daily, and it continues to be unhealthy. But put them into a clean, wheat and sugar-free body, and the damage shows up loud and clear!

Although I have never eaten wheat, after its elimination, I have indulged in foods containing refined sugar and lived to regret it. I thought it would be ok and that a little bit of sugar wouldn't hurt. But it did. I'd have a little bit more, which led to a little bit more. Before I knew it, I was hooked again. And what a difference it made to my Empath traits and health. It was like I suddenly became an antenna for negativity. I constantly felt crappy, low and overly Sensitive. And because I'd reignited the sugar addiction, I didn't want to give it up, even though I felt rubbish.

When I again removed refined sugar from my diet, the dark cloud lifted.

From time to time, I may end up consuming refined sugar, when out or at a party, but I am vigilante of not allowing myself to have it more than that once.

I would never risk eating wheat again, as I consider it to be more addictive and destructive to health than refined sugar and therefore just not worth the gamble.

10

Gluten and Food Intolerance

So far, I have discussed sugar and wheat, and the many damaging effects they have on the body and mind, but what about gluten?

Gluten is a protein found in wheat, barley and rye and, through cross-contamination, oats. It is gluten that gives bread its spongy, fluffy texture, and pizza its doughy stretchiness. But it is also gluten that can cause emotional sensitivities and a malfunctioning immune system.

After being wheat free for 4 weeks you should feel incredible in both your wellbeing and Sensitivities. However, if you have only seen slight improvements there is a strong possibility you are gluten intolerant (or have autoimmune disorder, leaky gut, or are menopausal more on that shortly).

Gluten Sensitivity

Once wheat is out of the body (the main source of gluten), gluten intolerance is very easy to pinpoint.

Signs of intolerance show up within 10 to 48 hours after eating foods or drinks that include gluten: rye, barley and oats (and wheat). Symptoms can be emotional or physical and can range from: depression, mood overload, anger, being excessively sensitive to people and their energy, bloating, fatigue, stomach cramps, indigestion, skin eruptions, headaches, sore throat, flu-like symptoms, constipation or diarrhea.

> *Food allergies show up quickly, either immediately or within hours of eating the offending food.*
>
> *Food intolerances show up slowly, normally within 10 to 48 hours.*

The most common misconception with gluten is if there are no bowel problems there is no intolerance. When in fact gastrointestinal symptoms are the least common presentation of gluten intolerance.

According to Dr Tom O'Bryan, known as the Sherlock Holmes of chronic disease and metabolic disorders who specializes in gluten intolerances, as many as seven out of ten people are gluten sensitive and most are unaware that their health problems are linked with it.

O'Bryan's testimony is becoming more accepted, as many are finding their health issues clear up when they give up gluten (or just wheat).

At this time, the best way to discover if you are gluten intolerant is through elimination, because blood tests are unreliable and inconclusive.

Dr Richard Hagmeyer, from the Naperville Institute, claims that at least 70% of gluten sensitivities go undetected. The reason for this is the tests used by the majority of healthcare practitioners are inaccurate. Here's why:

Gluten is 1 of 23'000 different proteins found in wheat. When being tested for gluten intolerance, only one or two factions (proteins) of gluten are tested, but there are hundreds more the human body can react to. It is for this reason, after tests, many people are told they are ok to eat gluten or wheat, when it is actually destroying their health and reducing their life expectancy!

The best way to diagnose a gluten intolerance is through abstinence. After following the 4-week wheat elimination plan, most sources of gluten will have been eliminated from your diet. As already mentioned, if you are gluten intolerant and you eat barley, rye, contaminated oats or wheat, you will get an adverse reaction within 48 hours.

The most commonly known illness associated with gluten is celiac disease, an autoimmune disease of the gut. Celiac goes hand-in-hand with a leaky gut.

A leaky gut means that certain proteins (like gluten) only get partially digested before leaking out of the gut lining into the bloodstream, causing major health problems.

Dr Hagmeyer believes most illness, of the body and mind, can be traced back to gluten intolerance. Gastrointestinal symptoms are the least common presentations of gluten sensitivity. The primary indications are neurological symptoms such as: depression, migraines, chronic headaches, vertigo, epilepsy, Parkinson's, ADD and ADHD. The second are hormone-related troubles and thirdly, autoimmune disease.

If you are intolerant, your body sees gluten as an invader and produces antibodies to attack it. However, it won't just attack the gluten. Other proteins that appear similar in structure, including the endocrine glands, are also attacked, and this is how autoimmune diseases develop.

There are at least 55 diseases associated with gluten intolerance and hundreds of symptoms that go with them. These symptoms, that manifest in many ways, come and go over the years. With each passing year they worsen and become a greater health risk. Too many people assume if they don't have a reaction immediately after eating certain foods, they are not problematic, which is why they don't recognize the link between their health problems and their diet.

Sensitive people tend to blame their heightened Sensitivities, such as overwhelm, depression and emotional vulnerability, on spending too much time around other humans, when they can be caused or worsened by food intolerance.

Undiagnosed food intolerances will almost always contribute to leaky gut and autoimmune disorders. Generally, wherever there is an autoimmune disease there will be leaky gut syndrome.

With leaky gut there is an increase in permeability of the intestinal lining, and large gaps form between the cells of the colon. These gaps allow undigested food particles, proteins and bacteria into the bloodstream. When these toxins get into the blood, the immune system kicks-in to attack them, but often ends up attacking the glands of the body as well, triggering autoimmune disease.

Autoimmune disease is becoming a 21st century curse with more and more people being diagnosed. The disease is caused by the immune system losing the ability to differentiate between proteins belonging to your own body (like the organs, glands, joints and muscles), and proteins belonging to a foreign invader such as bacteria, viruses and parasites.

There are varying factors in developing autoimmune disease but one of the known triggers is stress and emotional overload. It is this factor which makes those who are Sensitive more susceptible.

Autoimmune disorders are difficult to diagnose (it can take years to get an accurate diagnosis). The symptoms can be similar from one autoimmune disease to another. Here are some types you may have heard of: Psoriasis, Rheumatoid arthritis, type 1 diabetes, Hashimoto's thyroiditis, Graves' disease and Lupus, there are many more.

Autoimmune disease can cause leaky gut syndrome and vice versa.

What Causes Leaky Gut?

The most common causes of leaky gut are: stress, emotional overload, antibiotics and medications, Candida, alcohol, allergies, celiac disease, gluten and wheat intolerance, parasites, diet, and autoimmune disease.

Once you have a leaky gut and autoimmunity, there are many foods that trigger adverse reactions. These reactions can be anything from depression to joint pain. Wheat and refined sugar are high on the list for triggering an attack. Here are some others: all grains, gluten, dairy, eggs, nuts and seeds, all legumes (including soya), alcohol, potatoes, eggplants, tomatoes, chilies, coffee and processed foods.

Many Empaths and HSPs are vegetarian by choice, but it is vegetarian foods that cause the most havoc with emotional and physical health, if a leaky gut is present. That is not to say pulses, nuts, and nightshades are unhealthy, they're not. It is the reaction their exclusive form of lectins and proteins have within the leaky gut that cause the problems.

Revealing Signs

If you work to balance the mind, body and spirit, and have removed wheat and sugar from your diet, yet still suffer with depression or physical ailments, consider the possibility you may have food intolerances, a leaky gut and or autoimmune disorder. If this is the case your Sensitive traits will be heightened and you will be more open to other people's negative energy until you find balance.

Autoimmune can be diagnosed by a specialist or a good functional medicine practitioner. Once you have removed wheat and refined sugar from your diet, you are quickly able to see if other foods are causing undesirable reactions (remember the muddy water analogy).

Stress is a trigger for leaky gut and autoimmune flare-ups, this leaves the Sensitive vulnerable because they process other people's stress as well as their own.

We are all here for a reason and each have a purpose to fulfil. If we are being poisoned by the food we eat, we will never reach our true potential, nor will we ever get to grips with our Sensitive traits. The fear, anxiety, brain fog, intense fatigue, depression and emotional overload, certain foods cause (on top of all the 'Sensitive stuff') hold us back. If we don't have the energy or inclination to take part in any kind of life-fulfilling role, we certainly won't have the drive to reach it.

The good news is if you suffer food intolerances, leaky gut or autoimmune disorder you see life-changing results by removing trigger foods from your diet.

Most specialists working in this field agree: if you resist giving up certain foods it is likely you are intolerant to them. If you want to know what to eliminate, it will be that which you think you cannot live without. Addictive foods cause the worst health problems. As well as wheat and sugar, I was also resistant to giving up potatoes. I could not imagine life without them. But the cleaner my diet got the more I understood what a problem they were for me. Whenever I ate them, I would suffer bouts of depression or fatigue for a few days after consumption. It also heightened my negative Empath traits, leaving me more open to other people's emotional energy.

Trail of (Wheat-Free) Breadcrumbs

If you find, once you are wheat and sugar free, you get cravings for foods or if you start feeling unwell after eating certain vegetarian proteins or nightshades, you will likely have leaky gut. The best way to uncover if you have food intolerances is by firstly removing wheat and sugar from the diet.

If you want to learn more about autoimmune disorder, leaky gut or food intolerances I recommend you pay a visit to either autoimmune-paleo.com or paleomom.com where you will find a wealth of information on trigger foods and how to get tested for leaky gut.

Many women at the peri-menopausal stage of life are diagnosed with food intolerances, autoimmune and other health conditions. The subject of menopause goes beyond the scope of this book, but as it can cause many problems, I want to touch on it briefly. It is often at this stage of life that the 'elastic band' snaps for many women. And what I mean by this is, underlying health conditions that have been building over the years are suddenly revealed, by the extreme shift in hormones. These changes can start from the late thirties onwards, although most women suffer in their mid-to-late forties. There are too many symptoms to list here, but if you are in the age bracket, and you have eliminated wheat and sugar and you still have mood swings, brain fog or other symptoms, peri-menopause could be the reason.

11

4-Week Elimination Plan

The only way for you to discover the miracle of wheat and sugar elimination is to try it for yourself. It is one thing reading about the amazing results those, who are Sensitive, have felt following its removal, but it is not until you too experience it that you get to understand what all the fuss is about.

Seeing is believing!

If in doubt whether you can give wheat and sugar up for life, try going without it for 4 weeks. Tell yourself, if after 4 weeks you feel and look no different, your addictions have not gone or if you are still desperately craving bread, pizza and pasta, you can always go back to eating it again. I doubt you will, especially when you see the changes in yourself. And besides, you can still have all the above, just not made from wheat or refined sugar.

The Gift of Four Weeks Wheat and Sugar Free

I too didn't believe I could give them up. I expected I would go back to eating wheat once my allotted 4 weeks were up. But once out of my system, I saw exactly what Dr William Davies was talking about with his claims of wheat's addictive properties! And seeing the incredible change in myself was all it took to keep me off the evil grain! I believe so much in the power of diet changes that I make reference to it in every self-help book I write.

If your Empath or Sensitive traits have been out of hand for a long time, and you have been struggling to stay in emotional balance, after wheat and sugar's elimination you will see a huge change. Not only will you learn to navigate and understand your traits but you become happier and healthier too.

It is said that it takes sixty-six days for a new habit to form, or for an old one to die. But for most, it only takes 4 weeks for the wheat and sugar habit to have completely subsided. Within that time, you also see a shift in your happiness and emotional wellbeing. Some see a change after a few days, for others it may take weeks, but you will see a difference in the way you look, think and feel.

Yes, there is a chance you may get wheat and sugar withdrawal within the first week or two of elimination, which could be uncomfortable. You have to prepare mentally for this and keep telling yourself that it will soon pass. Believe me, any discomfort you experience is so worth enduring once through the other side.

Eat Real Food

Going wheat and sugar free does not mean eating food that tastes or looks like cardboard. Nor does it mean your diet is boring. What you can eat is delicious and satisfying. Your taste buds are no longer hijacked by chemicals and mind-altering substances, so real food becomes exquisite to the palate. You gain taste freedom and you will be amazed how delicious real food can taste when it does not contain so much as a grain of wheat or refined sugar.

The benefits of giving up wheat and sugar just keep on unfolding. Once they are out of the system, and you are over the addiction, you are not tempted into eating them again.

When you become liberated from wheat and sugar, don't be tricked into believing that now you no longer crave them you can have them every now and again. Unfortunately, that is not how this works. Wheat and sugar act like drugs. They fool your mind into believing you are in control of your choices. Just a little will hurt. It leads to a little bit more and a little bit more. Addictions always lie quietly in wait for their chance to be reborn.

When wheat is out of your life it means most refined sugar will be too. They go hand-in-hand. Where you find one you find the other. Even in savory breads. I believe wheat is worse than sugar in its quiet addictive nature and it is wheat that you have to stay most vigilante of avoiding.

If you want to do anything successfully you need to have a plan and stick to it. Fail to prepare and prepare to fail! Trying wheat elimination half-heartedly is not worth attempting. Not even its reduction by 80%. You will not see the complete benefits and even if you do, wheat will still be in your system and your addiction active. This means that your wheat consumption slowly but surely creeps back up. Before you know it, you are back binging on the stuff and the thought of giving wheat up again is even harder to face.

Yes, a little bit will hurt!

Those who I have seen fail, when attempting wheat elimination, are those who tell themselves 'a little won't hurt!' A slither of cake at a party, some breadcrumbs on the mozzarella sticks or a small slice of pizza on Saturday night will prevent you from beating the addiction. The desire to consume is not eradicated. And because of this you start to believe you have no willpower and cannot or do not want to give wheat up. Again, this is the power of wheat's addictive nature!

Anything that activates the opiate receptors in the brain, like wheat and sugar does, causes addiction and has to be avoided forever.

Excuses, Excuses

One excuse I hear a lot is that people are so busy they don't have time to prepare meals. I understand how busy people's lives are, and that is why I have set up the 4-week elimination plan for you to follow. The plan is here at your fingertips, so all you have to do is shop for ingredients and prep your meals. I devised the recipes to be no fuss and fast. It takes less time to whip them up than it does to order a take-away. It does not take long to throw some ingredients into a blender and into the oven, to beat up some eggs or toss together delicious salad ingredients. Making double or triple the amount means you can refrigerate or freeze for a later date. I also have some great tips that will help the transition into a wheat and sugar-free lifestyle.

I believe the reason it is difficult to contemplate wheat and sugar elimination is because of the lack of culinary inspiration. We live in a world where we have toast for breakfast, a sandwich for lunch and pizza, pasta or pie

100

for evening meal. Because we are all so busy, when we want to eat, we don't want to spend half an hour pondering our meal. This is where the program works. There are many easy-to-make amazing meal options and the inspiration is already here.

When starting the elimination program choose a month when you don't have much on. December, for example, is not a good month to start... unless you don't celebrate Christmas. Nor are the vacation months. Why? Because you need constant access to wheat and sugar-free food. If attending a Christmas celebration, whilst in withdrawal, where there is nothing but sandwiches, pastries and cakes on offer, and hunger strikes, I guarantee you will cave and eat something that contains the forbidden grain. This takes you back to square one. If it happens more than once, the elimination process becomes a brutal procedure.

You only notice the vast abundance of wheat and sugar within the world's fare when you decide to give it up! Keep the girl guide motto in your head at all times: "Be prepared!", it makes this transition a painless and successful one.

Being overcome with the need to feast on sugary or wheat treats isn't about having zero willpower or being weak-willed, it is about overcoming addiction and hard-wired eating habits, and a battle with brain chemistry. But it is a battle that can be easily won by following some simple steps.

Family Matters

It helps if the whole family does the plan together, especially if you are the one who prepares the meals. But if you suspect there is no way the rest of the family will willingly stop eating the evil grain, you may have to be a little sneaky. Give the family wheat-free meals without pointing it out to them. Chances are they won't even notice.

When other family members see the changes that happen in the way you look and feel, they are often only too willing to give it a try.

Now without further ado let's take a look how this program works:

The 4-Week Elimination Plan

Here are the guidelines for the plan. If you follow them, you will succeed in wheat and sugar elimination easily; and soon be on the path to emotional freedom, weight-loss, health and happiness:

1. **Eliminate wheat and sugar from your life for the four-week duration, and this means entirely**! If you are going to do this, you may as well do it properly. If you just reduce the amount of wheat and sugar in your diet, you will not see or reap the incredible benefits and you will still be addicted to them. After the four weeks are up, you will be amazed that you have no desire to eat either of them.

2. **Remember to read all labels.** Wheat and sugar are hidden everywhere! You will be surprised to see how many foods that actually contain them. I even found wheat in a brand of cream cheese. It's the same with sugar. Also, the higher they are up on the ingredients list, the higher the content.

3. **During elimination stage there are no wheat or gluten-free food replacements allowed**! This is super important! Free-from breads, cakes and biscuits

are strictly off the menu, especially until you have removed the wheat addiction. The reason for this is they are usually high in sugar and chemicals and are also, in themselves, addictive. Avoiding gluten-free replacements also breaks the habit of eating bread at each meal. Those who replaced bread, cakes and biscuits, etc. with store bought wheat or gluten-free replacements tend to put weight on and don't see many health benefits or improvements with their Sensitive traits. They also don't succeed in sugar elimination. Eating these gluten-free foods is like eating refined sugar. The body believes it is still getting its sugar-fix and the addiction still remains. In fact, gluten-free foods are higher on the glycemic index than the white sugar and wheat they are replacing!

A good thing to have on hand, during the four-week elimination, is oat cakes. They go great with soups and your favorite toppings.

Once wheat is out of the system, it is ok to occasionally include gluten-free replacement foods. This certainly makes dining out in restaurants easier.

4. Eat real food. Avoid anything processed. Keep your food as close to the way nature intended as possible. No low-fat or low-calorie, or foods that are laden with chemicals. Eat full-fat butter, lard, unprocessed coconut and olive oil, use double cream and full-fat mayonnaise. Having small amounts of the real thing is a hundred times better than eating large amounts of low-fat fake-food replacements.

5. **Choose organic dairy, fruit and veg.** By doing so it makes a vast difference to health and emotional wellness. The chemicals used for spraying non-organic produce acts like neuro-toxins, this in itself causes emotional and physical sensitivities. Not only does organic fruit and veg taste delicious, they are nutrient powerhouses.

6. If you eat meat, try to choose organic grass-fed. Over eighty percent of all produced antibiotics are given to livestock, and there can be up to twenty different medications present in non-organic meat and dairy.

It is also worth noting that many Empaths feel the energy of an animal within the meat. If the animal suffered or felt much fear before being slaughtered, it can trigger depression and low emotions in the Empath. The bigger the animal the more this energy is felt. If you find you are affected in this way, steering clear of meat may be the best option.

7. Avoid trans-fats and anything refined. Table salt and margarine being the worst culprits. They overload the body and are toxic to the system. However, your body needs salt (especially if you sweat heavily or drink large amounts of water), so instead of using the refined stuff, opt for unrefined sea or rock salt.

8. Avoid artificial sweetener such as Aspartame. If you wish to sweeten something use dark unrefined sugar, honey, maple syrup, xylitol or stevia.

9. Try to avoid eating carbs alone, especially if you want to lose weight. Carbohydrates (anything that has grown from the ground, e.g. potatoes, rice, fruit, etc.) break down into sugars in the bloodstream when digested; some much faster than others. Constant high blood sugars keep the sugar addiction alive and contribute to excess belly fat.

To slow down the absorption rate of carbs, eat them with some protein or fat. For example: an apple and a handful of almonds, or pineapple and cheese.

10. Be prepared! When out and about, going to friends, work or anywhere, take snacks in case you get hungry. Raw nuts are brilliant for this as they are both balanced (protein, carbohydrate and fat) and filling.

The best way to stay prepared is by having a food preparation day, and the weekend is the perfect time for this. On these days, bake your breads and muffins, and peel, cook and mash veg, all for the freezer. It is also a good time to plot out what you will eat each day and then shop accordingly. Having a good supply of foods that you can grab and go or have to quell a mid-afternoon hunger pang, is essential if you want to succeed on any eating plan.

11. Eat three meals a day and a couple of snacks. When you decide to break a food addiction, your body starts looking at ways to find its fix. You might find you want to eat when you're not hungry. This can lead to binge eating and a temptation to consume wheat or sugar. Try to have snacks containing protein, which help prevents sugar spikes. Pack your meals with as many nutrients as you can, in the form of healthy proteins and fats, fresh veg, salads and fruit. This keeps you full for longer and prevents unnecessary cravings.

Also, if you want to lose weight, eat only when hungry. Chew food slowly and stop eating when comfortably full, but not stuffed. You do your body no favors by over-feeding it, even with the good stuff! If you are still hungry twenty minutes after eating, you can always have some more.

~

You can choose from the breakfast, lunch and dinner options. Or if you would rather come up with your own wheat and sugar-free recipes, no problem. Just remember to follow the above guidelines when preparing them. If you want to have a breakfast for dinner or a dinner for lunch, feel free. The choice is yours.

When the 4 Weeks are Up

Now that you are wheat and sugar free you should be feeling fantastic! Your skin should be glowing and youthful, your clothes a little (or a lot) looser, your energy levels boosted and your happiness increased. Your brain should be clearer and your Sensitive traits more balanced and under control.

If feeling only marginally better do not panic. You may still be in the withdrawal period. For some it can go on for up to 12 weeks, although it is rare. Do not allow this to tempt you into eating wheat or sugar again. You have done the hardest part.

Also, if you don't yet feel great, it is a good idea to start keeping a food diary. If intolerant to certain foods now is the time you will see it. By taking note of what you eat, you will find a pattern in those foods causing reactions. You couldn't see or feel those intolerances before. But now you are clean from drug-like foods, you very quickly recognize when something does not agree with your system.

Should you find yourself suffering symptoms it is a good idea to reread Gluten and Food Intolerance in chapter 10.

Changing your diet really will change your life as a Sensitive. You never truly understand what drug-like food do to your mind, body and spirit until you remove them from your diet.

When making changes, listen to your intuition and not to the addiction. You can do it. You will succeed and get to become the best version of yourself

12

Wheat and Sugar-Free Cooking

When it comes to wheat and sugar-free baking, the process does take some getting used to. Although you can enjoy delicious baked goods, where you don't miss the wheat or sugar, the end results sometimes vary.

Wheat flour performs a range of different functions: it binds, thickens, absorbs moisture, changes texture and gives rise to bread. No single alternative can replicate all these tasks and this is why, in wheat-free baking, several flours are employed.

Flours that don't contain gluten do not have the same bind. Eggs, however, produce similar binding results in breads and cakes. In pastries, cheese is often used as the binder: cream cheese for sweet pastry and hard cheese for savory. Gelatin is often used by those following a low-carb diet. The most popular binder, in gluten-free products, is xanthan gum (an article published in the British Journal of Nutrition found xanthan gum to be safe, but recommended a limit of 15 grams a day, to prevent loose bowels. One serving is usually less than half a gram).

Loss of moisture is also common in gluten-free baking, but this can be improved by adding oil, honey, natural yogurt or buttermilk to recipes.

Because gluten-free baked goods quickly lose moisture, it is important to cover and store them soon after cooling. Store in an airtight container in the fridge or freeze once cooled.

Depending on what part of the world you live, your oven type and temperature and the quality of ingredients, will determine your end results in gluten-free baking. The more time you spend baking, the more you get to understand the different flours. You can then refine and tweak recipes to better work for you.

Although I have given some oven temperatures to bake at, if you find you don't get good results with your cakes and breads, refer to your oven manufacture's guidelines for baking temperatures and cooking times. If a recipe within this book suggests to bake for 10 minutes, check it after 8, or if it calls for a 45-minute bake check after 30 minutes. You will soon get used to the different flours and how long they take to bake in your own oven.

I am a very basic baker. Meaning, I like everything to be as simple as possible. When you come to the recipes, you will find them uncomplicated. If I can get away with the all-in technique (everything in the blender and mixed), that's what I'll do.

Measurements

For ease, I have done most measurements in cup sizes. When short on time it is much easier to use a cup for measuring, rather than using the weighing-scales. In some recipes I have used weight measurements when they need to be more specific, or if what is being measured is difficult to weigh in a cup. If you don't have a measuring cup, a tea cup is ok to use.

Measuring cups are cheap to buy and are worth the investment. They normally come in packs of four: 1, ¾, ½ and ¼ cup measurements.

Wheat Replacement Flours and How to Use Them:

Ground Almonds: Ground almonds (also known as almond meal) are a must in any wheat-free kitchen and can be used in almost any cake, biscuit, muffin, bread or pizza base, with perfect results. Almonds are full of healthy monounsaturated fats and proteins and can do most things wheat flour can, but won't cause blood sugar spikes or addictions.

Almond Flour: The flour is more finely milled than ground almonds, and will give different results in baking. Being a different texture and product, it is wise not to confuse the two in recipes.

Coconut Flour: Coconut flour has a light texture and is great for making sweet or savory muffins and cakes, but can take some getting used to. It absorbs a lot of fluid and a little goes a long way. Half a cup is all that's needed to make 6 good sized muffins. The texture of the muffin batter tends to be thicker than other wheat/gluten-free flours.

If too runny, coconut flour batter will not bake through properly, no matter how long your muffins are in the oven. As a general rule: to every half a cup of coconut flour add 3 eggs and ½ cup of fluid. As every batch is often different, more or less fluid may be needed.

Coconut flour is high in fiber and low in carbohydrates, making it great for a low-carb plan.

Chickpea Flour (Gram or Besan): When going wheat free, chickpea flour often becomes a store-cupboard staple. It can be used to make delicious pancakes, savory breads, cakes and muffins. It is an economical flour that works especially well when mixed with almond meal or other ground nuts.

Ready-Mixed Gluten-Free Flours: Although there are recipes using gluten-free flours in this book, it is best to use them sparingly or have occasionally if used alone. They are mostly made up from ground rice, potato or tapioca starch which turn to sugar quickly within the body.

Flaxseed Flour: Ground flaxseeds have a strong nutty flavor. Flaxseed flour is also known as ground linseeds or flax meal. It is a great addition for bread making, giving a fluffy texture and wheaty flavor. It is nutritious, low-carb and high fiber.

Millet Flour: Millet is sweet in flavor and often used for muffins and flatbreads. It is similar in color to polenta.

Soya Flour: Often used in low-carb baking and cooking, soya flour is best used in conjunction with other wheat-free flours.

Buckwheat Flour: Contrary to what the name may suggest, buckwheat is not a form of wheat, it is derived from the rhubarb family and is completely wheat and gluten-free. Buckwheat has the texture and taste of a grain and works well in many wheat-free baking recipes. It also makes great blini pancakes. Buckwheat has a low GI factor and won't spike blood sugar levels.

Polenta Flour/Corn Meal: This can be used in muffins and breads. It provides color, flavor and increases moisture content. I find it makes the best muffins when mixed with ground almonds. It has a higher GI than some other flours so should be used sparingly.

Arrowroot: Arrowroot is mostly used as a thickener for gravies and sauces but it can also be used in bread-making. Mix it into a paste with water before adding to sauces.

Cornflour: Another thickening agent that works the same as arrowroot is cornflour, which is made from finely ground corn. It is also known as corn starch.

Sugar Replacements

If choosing a sweetener to cook with or to add to drinks, opt for small amounts of dark unrefined sugar, organic honey or maple syrup.

For baking, unsweetened pureed dried fruit makes an excellent sugar replacement as does honey and maple syrup. The only other sweeteners I would recommend using is stevia or xylitol.

Stevia: Being 300 times sweeter than sugar, stevia is derived from the leaf of the stevia plant. It comes in both granulated and liquid form.

Xylitol: A natural sugar alcohol that can be digested by our bodies. Xylitol is derived from fruits, vegetables, corn husks and hardwood, and works well in cooking and baking. It comes in granulated form.

Avoid: It is important to avoid aspartame and any other artificial sweeteners. They are toxic, indigestible and carcinogenic.

Looking Out for Hidden Wheat

If a food label states any of these items are included in the ingredients, it contains wheat:

- Wheat/whole-wheat
- Wheat bran, wheatgerm or wheat starch
- Breadcrumbs
- Bulger
- Cereal extract
- Couscous
- Farina
- Flour
- Wholemeal flour
- Wheat flour
- Modified starch
- Semolina
- Spelt
- Kamut
- Vegetable protein
- Vegetable gum
- Vegetable starch

Tips for a Wheat and Sugar-Free Life

Now that you have done the hard part, and gone through withdrawal, you want to make sure you never go have to through it again. Here are some excellent tips to keep you wheat and sugar free forever:

Be Prepared:

When out and about, going to friends, work or anywhere take snacks in case you get hungry. Nuts are brilliant for this. They are healthy, balanced and filling.

Try to have your nuts raw and unsalted. Roasting them kills many of their nutrients, and the added salt will normally be refined.

Bake and Freeze:

When baking wheat-free breads, muffins or pizza bases, make more than needed so you can freeze for a later date. Choose one day a week or month and do all your baking on that day. Simply double up the ingredients on the recipes.

Make Wheat-Free Breadcrumbs:

When cooking from scratch, wheat-free breadcrumbs are handy to have in the freezer for making fish cakes, sausages or burgers.

To make breadcrumbs, pop stale or toasted wheat-free bread into a food processor and blitz till the bread becomes crumbs. Freeze in batches.

Read Labels:

Wheat and sugar are hidden in all sorts of foods; it is essential to check all labels. Wheat is a common allergen, so it will usually be highlighted in bold. Refined sugars can be disguised under many titles such as: glucose, fructose or corn syrup.

Don't Be Fooled into Thinking a Little Won't Hurt:

It only takes a small amount of wheat or refined sugar to reignite the addiction and it only takes a tiny amount of wheat to create a negative bodily reaction.

A slither of cake here or a biscuit there may seem harmless but it will put you on a fast-tracked-path back to being a wheat and sugar addict. This is why it is essential to be prepared when out and about. If hunger strikes and the only foods available contain wheat or sugar, it is too easy to give into hunger and eat the drug-like food. We have to remember these so-called foods create a dependence.

A drug addict could not get off drugs if she had a little high here or there, nor could the alcoholic if he had the odd glass of wine. To get rid of an addiction we have to stay away from the cause.

Keep Your Diet Varied:

Feeling bored or restricted by your diet can lead to being tempted to snack on a sugary or wheat treat. Keeping your diet varied will prevent food boredom and help you avoid temptation. Especially in the early days of elimination. Stay inspired by trying out new recipes for meals and snacks, or try foods you would not normally eat.

Phone Ahead When Eating Out:

There is nothing worse than getting to a restaurant to discover the only thing you can eat is fries and a side salad.

Numerous establishments now cater for special dietary requirements, but it is advisable to phone ahead first. Many eateries will allow you to bring along your own bread, pasta or pizza bases if they do not have wheat or sugar-free options.

Keep Your Cupboards Well Stocked:

Always keep in a good stock of wheat-free and sugar-free cooking ingredients: Fresh fruit and veg, eggs, seeds, nuts, ground almonds, wheat-free flours, unrefined sweeteners, honey or maple syrup, pulses, herbs and spices, rice, rice noodles and oats, etc., so you can easily whip up snacks, treats or meals.

Use Honey, Stevia, Xylitol, Maple Syrup, Dried Fruit or Dark Unrefined Sugar in Cooking:

These natural sweeteners not only add a delicious sweetness to your dishes but also have nutritional value.

Keep Stevia Sweeteners with You at all Times:

If you are one who likes to have sweetness in your beverages, stevia or xylitol is a good replacement and a much healthier option than having aspartame sweeteners.

Ok, onto the recipe section...

Section 2

13

Recipes and Meal Ideas

Breakfasts

1. Banana and almond smoothie   119
2. Di's ultimate smoothie   120
3. Blueberry and coconut muffins   122
4. Savory omelet   124
5. Sweet berry omelet   126
6. Strawberries and cream smoothie   127
7. Banana bread   128
8. Breakfast bars   130
9. Oats your way   132
10. Oat cakes   134
11. Fruit and yogurt   136
12.Toast with 10 types of toppings   137
13. Eggs on protein pancakes   138

1 Banana and Almond Smoothie

This simple yet delicious smoothie can be enjoyed at any time, but is especially beneficial to the body at the start of the day. It is good a balance of fat, protein and carbohydrate.

> *Health Bite*
>
> *Almonds are tiny nutrient powerhouses that should be eaten regularly to reap their amazing health benefits.*

Ingredients

Serves 2

- 1 medium-sized banana
- 2 tbsp. ground almonds
- 1 cup, full-fat, natural yogurt
- 1 tbsp. honey
- ½ cup milk
- 2 tbsp. double cream
- ice (optional)

Instructions

- ❖ Place all the ingredients, except the double cream, into a blender and whizz up for a few seconds.
- ❖ Add the cream and blend again for a few seconds, until smooth and creamy. Serve immediately

2 Di's Ultimate Breakfast Smoothie

This smoothie is the perfect way to start your day. It is filling, keeping hunger at bay for hours, and both delicious and nutritious. Taking mere seconds to whip up, this breakfast smoothie is soothing and healing to your gut, and helps prevent illness of the digestive tract.

> *Health Bite*
>
> *Packed with live nutrients, fiber, healthy fats, protein and low GI carbs makes this the ultimate healing meal. It contains both prebiotics (prunes and banana) and probiotics (yogurt) which encourage the colon's good bacteria to thrive. It aids in gut healing and offers great digestive health. Because it calms the gut, it also helps calm anxiety and stress.*

Ingredients

2 servings

- ➤ 1 medium banana
- ➤ 4 prunes
- ➤ Handful of raw macadamia nuts or almonds
- ➤ 1 cup hulled mixed berries (strawberries, raspberries and blueberries)
- ➤ 2 tbsp. live organic yogurt
- ➤ 1 tbsp. raw coconut oil
- ➤ 1 tbsp. double cream
- ➤ ½ cup cold filtered water (if smoothie is to thick add more water)
- ➤ 3 ice cubes (optional)

Instructions

❖ Simply pop all the ingredients into a Nutri-bullet or other powerful blender (that can blend nuts and ice) and whizz up for 30 seconds.

❖ Eat immediately or put in a flask to enjoy later.

3 Blueberry and Coconut Muffins

Perfect for a breakfast on the run or afternoon snack, these yummy blueberry muffins are not only sugar, wheat, gluten and grain-free but low GI, low-carb, high fiber and, most importantly, delicious!

> *Health Bite*
>
> *Coconut flour is high in fiber, low-carb and low GI. Meaning it won't spike your blood sugars. When used following a low GI or low-carb diet, coconut flour aids in shedding excess weight. Being so high in fiber, it keeps you full for longer.*

Ingredients for 6 Muffins

- ½ cup coconut flour
- 3 medium eggs
- ½ cup butter softened or raw coconut oil
- ½ cup granulated stevia (Truvia)
- ½ cup blueberries
- ½ cup milk (dairy, coconut or almond)
- ½ tsp baking powder

Instructions

- Whisk the eggs together with a hand mixer.
- Add the stevia, butter or oil, milk, baking powder and coconut flour and mix well, making sure there are no lumps.
- With a spoon, fold blueberries into the mixture.

❖ Divide mixture between 6 muffin cases then pop into a preheated oven and bake for 15 minutes or until muffins are well risen and firm to touch.
❖ Leave to cool on a wire rack.

4 Savory Omelet

Omelets are perfect for breakfast or brunch. Served with a salad or veg, they also make a perfect light dinner. They are both filling and nutritious and super-easy to whip up.

> *Health Bite*
>
> *Mushrooms are one of the best vegetable sources of selenium which is important for healthy skin and hair. It is also vital for proper thyroid function.*

Ingredients

Serves 1 to 2

- ½ onion, finely chopped
- ½ bell pepper, deseeded and diced
- ½ cup sliced mushrooms
- ¼ cup diced cooked ham (optional)
- 3 medium eggs
- 1 tbsp. double cream
- butter for cooking
- salt and pepper to taste

Instructions

- ❖ In a medium/large frying pan melt a small knob of butter on a medium heat, being careful not to burn the butter. Add the onions and toss around for a few minutes before adding mushrooms and bell peppers. Fry gently for 3 or 4 minutes until soft.
- ❖ Meanwhile in a medium bowl whip the eggs together with double cream, salt and pepper, and

diced ham, if using. Pour the softened vegetables into the egg mixture and stir in.

❖ Add another knob of butter to the frying pan to melt. Then pour in egg mixture. Cook until firm and golden underneath and top is starting to set. Transfer to a hot grill to brown the top.

❖ Serve immediately

5 Sweet Berry Omelet

This takes a different slant on the traditional savory omelet. It's great to have if you enjoy a sweet, fruity breakfast. It's quick to make and deliciously filling.

> *Health Bite*
>
> *This omelet is a perfect balance or protein carbohydrate and fat. The fresh berries provide vitamin C and antioxidants; eggs are packed with essential amino acids.*

Ingredients

Serves 1-2

- ➤ 2 medium eggs
- ➤ 1 to 2 tbsp. organic honey
- ➤ 1 tbsp. raw organic coconut oil
- ➤ ½ cup of mixed fresh berries (strawberries, raspberries or blueberries)
- ➤ Greek yogurt or mascarpone to serve

Instructions

- ➤ With a hand mixer whip up the eggs and honey.
- ➤ Melt the coconut oil in a small to medium frying pan.
- ➤ Drop the berries into the egg batter, give it a quick stir, pour into the pan and cook until golden brown underneath. Transfer the pan to a grill, to lightly brown the top.
- ➤ Serve with a dollop of Greek yogurt or mascarpone.

6 Strawberries and Cream Smoothie

This simple yet delicious smoothie can be enjoyed at any time, it can even be enjoyed as a dessert. To add more protein, simply add two tablespoons of almonds.

> *Health Bite*
>
> *Double cream has healthy fats, good amounts of protein, calcium, and phosphorus, and can help curb your mid-meal cravings.*

Ingredients

Serves 1

- ➢ 6 to 8 medium-sized strawberries, hulled
- ➢ 1 cup, full-fat, natural yogurt
- ➢ 1 tbsp. honey
- ➢ ¼ cup milk
- ➢ 2 tbsp. double cream
- ➢ ice (optional)

Instructions

- ❖ Place all the above ingredients, except the double cream, into a blender and whizz up for twenty seconds.
- ❖ Add the cream and blend again for a few seconds, until smooth and creamy. Serve immediately.

7 Banana Bread

This is a real wheat and sugar-free treat and one I'm sure you will want to bake regularly. It is ideal as a breakfast, at home or on the go, and is a perfect afternoon pick-me-up, served with a cup of tea.

> *Heath Bite*
>
> *Bananas are high in fiber and are prebiotic, meaning they help feed the good bacteria in the gut.*

Ingredients

4 to 6 servings

- ➤ 2 cups of ground almonds
- ➤ 1 tbsp. honey or granulated stevia
- ➤ 3 small or medium, ripe (browning) mashed bananas
- ➤ 3 large eggs
- ➤ 1 tsp baking powder (gluten-free)
- ➤ ¼ cup melted butter or melted coconut oil
- ➤ ½ tsp unrefined sea salt
- ➤ small bread tin lined with greaseproof paper, well-greased (mixture tends to stick)

Instructions

- ❖ Preheat the oven.

- ❖ Whip up eggs with blender or hand whisk until light and airy. Then add the rest of ingredients and mix into a smooth batter.
- ❖ Pour into the lined baking tin and bake for 50 to 60 mins or until firm to touch.
- ❖ Remove from tin and allow to cool on wire rack.
- ❖ Eat within 2 to 3 days

8 Breakfast Bars

Although labeled as breakfast bars, these are perfect to have at any time of the day when hunger strikes.

> *Health Bite*
>
> *Almonds are packed with vitamin E which is a powerful antioxidant. They are great for keeping hunger at bay and balancing blood sugars.*

Ingredients

8 to 12 servings

- ➢ 2 cups ground almonds (almond meal)
- ➢ ½ cup mixed dried berries (e.g. blackberry, blueberry, raspberry)
- ➢ 1 egg
- ➢ ½ cup dried, unsweetened, coconut
- ➢ ½ cup mixed seeds (sesame, sunflower, pumpkin)
- ➢ ¼ cup honey or granulated stevia
- ➢ 1 tsp baking powder
- ➢ 1 tsp vanilla essence
- ➢ 2 tbsp. raw coconut oil, melted

Instructions

- ❖ Preheat the oven to 200°C
- ❖ Mix all the above ingredients together in a bowl.

❖ Tear off 2 pieces of baking paper, the size of a small baking tray. Place mixture in the center of one sheet and cover with the other. Then using a rolling pin, roll out mixture to about an inch thick.

❖ Carefully peel off the top layer of paper and, using the underneath piece of greaseproof, place the rolled-out mixture onto a baking tray. Pop into the oven for 10 minutes.

❖ Using a pizza cutter or sharp knife, slice into the desired size, remove from parchment and allow to cool on a rack.

9 Oats

When I first gave up wheat and was getting away from my 'wheaty ways,' I found oats to be a life-saver. For breakfasts or lunch, I would often munch away on some form of the humble oat. And for this reason, I have added a page with ways to enjoy your oats (ahem) in some versatile ways.

Porridge

There are many ways to brighten up what could be described as bland dish. Make up the porridge following the pack instructions, add any of the following:

- Maple syrup and pecans
- Honey, almond slivers and double cream
- Cinnamon, honey and raisons
- Chopped prunes, crushed mixed nuts and honey
- Greek yogurt, honey and fresh berries

Oat Cakes

Store brought organic wheat and gluten-free oat cakes are great to have on hand They normally come in individually wrapped packets, which are perfect for taking to work for a breakfast on the run, light lunch or afternoon snack. You can also make your own. Top with any of the following:

- Goats cheese and beetroot
- Feta and rocket salad
- Cream cheese and cucumber
- Peanut butter and banana
- Avocado and tomato
- Cottage cheese and pineapple

- Sardine pâté
- Egg mayonnaise
- Cheddar and pear

10 Oat Cakes

These are quite different from what you buy in the shops but are equally as delicious.

Make sure the oatmeal is fresh, if not the oatcakes can taste bitter.

> Health Bite
>
> *Oats stimulate the production of serotonin, the feel-good hormone in the brain. They also contain several B vitamins which help promote nerve health and good mood.*

Ingredients

- ➤ 1 cup medium-cut oatmeal
- ➤ 1/3 cup boiling water
- ➤ 1/2 tsp unrefined sea salt
- ➤ 1 tsp butter
- ➤ gluten-free flour for dusting

Instructions

- ❖ Preheat the oven.
- ❖ Put oats in a medium bowl.
- ❖ Melt the butter and dissolve the salt in the boiling water, add to oatmeal and mix well.
- ❖ Allow the oats to swell for a minute or so.
- ❖ Split mix into two balls and turn out onto a floured pastry board. Using a rolling pin roll out one of the balls as thinly as possible.

- ❖ Using a cookie cutter or pizza slicer, cut out the cakes. Do the same with the other oat ball.
- ❖ Place on a baking sheet and bake in the oven until they are slightly golden and their edges starting to curl.
- ❖ Remove from oven and cool on a rack.
- ❖ Store in an airtight container.

11 Fruit and Yogurt

A delicious way to start the day. Having freshly chopped fruit will set you off on the right foot for an energized day. If short on time in the morning, prepare your fruit the night before and cover with freshly squeezed lemon juice to prevent it from browning.

> *Health Bite*
>
> *Packed with fiber, antioxidants and vitamin C, these fruits help guard against stress, keep a strong immune system and contribute to radiant, youthful looking skin.*

Ingredients

Serves 1

- ½ cup organic Greek yogurt
- 1 apple, chopped
- 1 kiwi, chopped
- 4 strawberries, hulled and chopped
- 1 banana, sliced
- ¼ cup blueberries
- toasted sunflower and sesame seeds
- drizzle of honey

Instructions

- ❖ Place all the fruit in a bowl, top with yogurt, seeds and honey.
- ❖ Serve immediately.

12 Toasts

I've lost count of the times people have said to me: 'You don't have wheat... what do you eat?' Most cannot begin to imagine a life without bread at every meal, starting with toast for breakfast.

Yes, you can still have toast! Albeit a different version than what you are used to. We still want soldiers to dip into our eggs and somewhere to slather our butter, but we don't want it at a cost to our health, happiness and wellbeing.

There are several different bread recipes in the bakery section, all ideal for toasting (although you are probably best toasting it under a grill as opposed to a toaster). You can play around with different varieties and find which you most prefer.

Here are 10 healthy and filling toppings:

- Peanut butter (sugar-free) and banana
- Melted cheese and tomato
- Cheddar cheese and Marmite
- Tuna pâté
- Peanut butter and sliced strawberries
- Sardine pâté
- Fried, scrambled or poached eggs
- Sardines in tomato sauce
- Sardines and avocado
- Mashed avocado, tomato and mozzarella

13 Eggs on Protein Pancakes

This high protein meal is great for breakfast or lunch. It is satisfying and delicious. Serve with a couple of grilled or fried tomatoes and you have a lovely balance of carbs, protein and fat. To save time (and washing up) you can cook the pancakes and eggs in the same frying pan at the same time. Just be sure to keep the pancakes small and cook on one side of the frying pan.

> *Health Bite*
>
> *Chickpeas are high in iron, an important antioxidant that maintains brain and blood health and energy levels.*

Ingredients

Serves 1

- ➢ 2 tbsp. gram flour (chickpea flour)
- ➢ 3 tbsp. water
- ➢ salt and pepper
- ➢ coconut oil or butter to cook
- ➢ 1 to 2 eggs

Instructions

- ❖ Put gram flour and water into a bowl or jug and whisk up. Season well.
- ❖ Heat oil in a large frying pan.

❖ Pour batter mixture in one or two thin pancake shapes, on one side of the pan, and fry for 1 to 2 minutes
❖ Crack eggs into frying pan, a small distance from the pancake, and cook as liked.
❖ Flip pancake to cook other side for a minute or two.
❖ Remove pancakes from the pan when browned, top with eggs and serve.

Lunch

1.Jacket potatoes with choice of toppings 141
2. Sandwiches 6 ways   142
3. Onion soup   144
4. Mushroom toasts   146
5. Buckwheat blinis   148
6. Cheesy dip and crudités   150
7. Olive flatbread and tuna pate   151
8. Creamy celery soup   153
9. Courgette and mint soup   162
10. Potato cakes   155
11.Spicy parsnip soup   156
12. Waldorf salad   158
13. Pea and mint soup   160
14. Greek salad   163

1 Jacket Potatoes

Potatoes cooked with their skins are a fantastic and filling meal, which are both easy to make and economical.

If you take your lunch to work, cook your jacket potatoes the evening before. Keep your topping separate and reheat the potato in a microwave.

You can have sweet or baking potatoes. If you suffer with bloating after eating normal potatoes, or if you want to lose weight, stick with sweet potatoes.

There are many yummy toppings to choose from, here's some to get you started:

Toppings

- **Tuna mayo**: 1 small tin of tuna mixed with 2 tbsp. organic mayonnaise and a tbsp. of sweetcorn.
- **Egg mayo**: 2 hardboiled eggs peeled mashed together with 2 tbsp. organic mayonnaise.
- **Cheddar and coleslaw**: Grate 2oz. Cheddar and top with creamy coleslaw
- **Coronation chicken**: Mix 2 tbsp. mayonnaise with 1 tbsp. mild curry powder, then add half a cup of cooked, chopped chicken.
- **Cottage cheese and chive**: top your potato with full-fat cottage cheese served with a snipping of fresh chopped chives.

2 Sandwiches

When going wheat-free, sandwiches may seem like a thing of the past, but it does not have to be.

Granted, wheat and gluten-free breads do not hold the same way, nor do they have the same rise, but the fillings that can be enjoyed are every bit as delicious.

Sandwiches are portable. Because these are made with high protein breads, they are very filling, even though their size is small.

I find the bread slices are often best toasted if being taken as part of a packed lunch.

Choose your favorite bread from the bakery section to slice.

Single Serving Sandwich Fillings

- **Ham and Cheese**: 1 slice ham, 1 slice Emmental cheese, 3 slices cucumber, 3 thin slices tomato, 1 tsp mustard, 1 tsp mayonnaise.
- **Corned Beef**: 1 thin slice corned beef, 1 slice Emmental cheese, 1 tbsp. sauerkraut, 1 tbsp. thousand island dressing.
- **Turkey and Brie**: 1 to 2 slices turkey, 2 thin slices tomato, 2 thin slices Brie, 2 tbsp. mayonnaise.
- **Avocado, Mozzarella and Tomato**: 3 to 4 slices avocado, 3 thin slices mozzarella cheese, 3 thin slices tomato, handful salad leaves, 1 tbsp. mayonnaise.
- **Cheese and Tomato**: 2 slices Cheddar cheese, 3 thin slices tomato, 1 tbsp. mayonnaise.

- **Prawn Cocktail**: small serving cooked prawns, 2 tbsp. thousand island dressing, handful rocket leaves, 3 slices cucumber.

3 Onion Soup

This will certainly warm your cockles on a cold day! The slow cooking process develops a lovely sweetness to the onions that makes this soup very moreish.

> *Health Bite*
>
> *Most people don't know but onions are one of the best sources of calcium other than dairy. They have properties that are antiviral, antibiotic and anti-inflammatory. Not everyone digests raw onions well and are often best eaten cooked.*

Ingredients

- 4 medium onions finely sliced
- 4 cloves of garlic minced
- 1 1/2 pints of hot wheat-free stock (preferably beef)
- 1 tbsp. organic honey
- unrefined sea salt and ground black pepper to season
- 2 tbsp. grated Parmesan cheese
- few thyme sprigs
- 2 tbsp. butter

Instructions

- ❖ In a medium-sized soup pan, gently heat the butter, after it stops sizzling add the onions and soften on a low heat for 10 mins, add garlic then leave to cook on a very low heat for 30 minutes. Stirring occasionally.

- ❖ Add the thyme sprigs cook for 3 minutes.
- ❖ Add the stock and honey, bring back to boil, cover, then simmer for 45 minutes. Stirring occasionally.
- ❖ Dish up, sprinkle over parmesan cheese and serve.

4 Mushroom Toasts

These mushroom toasts are easy to make, filling, nutritious and economical. They work well as a big breakfast or a light lunch.

> *Health Bite*
>
> *Mushrooms contain more protein than any other vegetable and are a great source of B12, which is particularly beneficial to those who eat little or no meat. They are packed with minerals, especially selenium*

Ingredients

Serves 1

- ➢ 1 cup chopped button mushrooms
- ➢ 1 cup milk (dairy or non-dairy)
- ➢ 1 tbsp. butter, plus extra for toast
- ➢ 2 tsp arrowroot or cornflour, mixed with a little milk into a thick but runny consistency
- ➢ unrefined sea salt and pepper
- ➢ 2 slices wheat-free bread

Instructions

- ❖ Place butter in a medium pan and melt.
- ❖ When butter stops sizzling put mushrooms in and toss around to coat evenly. Turn heat down and cook for 5 or 10 minutes on a low heat, until softened.
- ❖ Season well then add milk to pan and bring to the boil.

- ❖ Pour in arrowroot mix (or cornflour) whilst stirring continuously to ensure no lumps form. The sauce will immediately thicken.
- ❖ Turn heat down and simmer for 5 minutes, stirring occasionally.
- ❖ Meanwhile place bread under grill. When toasted sufficiently, butter, pour over creamed mushrooms and serve immediately.

5 Buckwheat Blinis

Buckwheat blinis are small fluffy pancakes traditionally served with caviar or smoked salmon. They are easy to make, much cheaper and more delicious than buying ready-made.

This blini recipe is a simple version that makes yummy light and fluffy pancakes, great as a lunch, snack or starter and can be served with savory or sweet toppings.

> *Health Bite*
>
> *Buckwheat has a low GI factor and won't spike blood sugar levels. It is high in magnesium which improves blood flow and allows for better nutrient distribution through the body.*

Ingredients

Serves 2 (if more required double or triple mixture)

> ➤ ¼ cup buckwheat flour
> ➤ ½ tsp gluten-free baking powder
> ➤ pinch salt
> ➤ 2 tbsp. milk (dairy or non-dairy)
> ➤ 1 egg
> ➤ olive oil to fry

Instructions

❖ Mix all dry ingredients together in a bowl or jug.

❖ Whisk eggs and milk together, in a separate bowl, add to dry mixture and whisk again to make a smooth paste.
❖ Heat oil and using a jug pour the batter in droplets (2 to 3-inch diameter) into the pan.
❖ Cook for about 45 seconds either side, or until golden.

6 Delicious Cheesy Dip and Crudités

When following a gluten-free or sugar-free lifestyle choosing snacks or a light lunch, to have on the go, or when in a hurry, can be tricky. This dip is also delicious when served with potato wedges, gluten-free tortilla chips or oat cakes.

> *Health Bite*
>
> *By eating veg raw it helps pack your body with valuable health-promoting, life-enhancing, anti-aging enzymes.*

Ingredients Serves 2 to 4

- ½ cup cream cheese
- ½ cup mayonnaise
- ½ cup of strong blue cheese, such as Roquefort or Stilton, crumbled
- choice of salad vegetables, such as celery, carrot and cucumber, chopped into batons

Instructions

- ❖ Simply place all ingredients (except veg) into a medium bowl and, using a hand blender, whip up into a creamy consistency.
- ❖ Serve immediately or chill until needed.

7 Olive Flatbread and Tuna Pâté

The combination of flavors in the olive flatbread and tuna pâté marry perfectly together. They are super-easy to make and work well as an appetizer, snack or light lunch. But be aware they are incredibly moreish...

Ingredients for the olive flatbread:

Makes 10 to 16 flatbread, depending on size.

- ➢ 2 cups wheat-free bread flour
- ➢ 1 cup milk (dairy or other)
- ➢ 1 tsp wheat-free baking powder
- ➢ 15 green pitted olives, chopped
- ➢ 1 tsp unrefined sugar

Instructions

- ❖ In a bowl, mix all the dry ingredients and the chopped olives. Gradually pour in the milk and using hands, mix until a pliable dough is formed (as all wheat and gluten-free flours vary, it is best to add the milk slowly. With some flours a cup of milk will not be enough, with others it will be too much).

- ❖ Place the dough on a floured board. The flatbread can either be shaped with hands or rolled out: take small clumps of the dough, roll in flour and flatten down with hands or roll out (this dough does not roll well when done in larger pieces, keeping the sections smaller works better). Using a large mug

151

or pastry cutter, cut out biscuit shaped flatbread. Continue this way till all the dough is used.

- ❖ Place in a preheated oven 180ºC for 8 to 12 minutes, till firm and slightly crisp on outside.
- ❖ Serve when warm.

Ingredients for the tuna pâté:

- ➤ 185g tin of tuna in oil or brine, drained
- ➤ 150g cream cheese (wheat-free)
- ➤ 2 tsp capers, drained
- ➤ 1 tsp lemon juice
- ➤ salt and pepper

Instructions

- ❖ Using a hand blender or food processor, simply whizz up all ingredients to a smooth, creamy consistency, season to taste.

Chill until required. Tuna pâté will last 3 days, covered in fridge. Flatbread are best frozen on day baked.

8 Creamy Celery Soup

Celery is a very underrated vegetable. It is mainly used raw in salads or as an accompaniment to dips, yet is equally delicious when cooked. This soup is satisfying, easy and economical to make.

> *Health Bite*
>
> *Not only has celery got many nutritional benefits it is also good for numerous nervous conditions. Hippocrates, known as the 'Father of Medicine', used celery in the treatment of nervous patients and modern research in China and Germany have found essential oils extracted from the celery seed, to have a calming effect on the central nervous system.*

Ingredients

makes 2-3 large servings

- 3 sticks of celery, peeled and finely chopped
- 1 medium onion, peeled and diced
- 1 potato, peeled and chopped into small chunks
- 2 to 3 tsp vegetable stock (depending on taste preference)
- 1/2 pint boiling water
- knob of butter
- 2 tbsp. double cream
- salt and pepper

Instructions

❖ Melt the butter in a medium-sized pan. After it stops sizzling, but before it turns brown, add the onions and toss around to cover them in butter. Turn the heat down and let them sweat for 5 minutes.

❖ Add in the rest of ingredients, except the double cream, stir together, bring to boil, then stir again. Turn heat down, cover and simmer for 20 minutes.

❖ Check with a fork that the potato and celery are soft and turn off heat. Add cream then blend soup to a smooth consistency. Season to taste.

9 Courgette and Mint Soup

Courgettes, also known as zucchini, are incredibly versatile and easy to cook with. This soup is quick to make and tastes delicious!

> **Health Bite**
>
> *Courgettes are high in vitamin C, antioxidants, vitamin E and omega 3 fatty acids, essential for brain health.*

Ingredients

> ➢ 1 medium onion, diced
> ➢ good handful of mint leaves finely chopped
> ➢ 1 ½ pints of hot gluten-free stock (chicken or veg)
> ➢ 2 large or 4 small courgettes, coarsely grated
> ➢ unrefined sea salt and ground black pepper
> ➢ splash of double or single cream
> ➢ large knob of butter

Instructions

> ❖ Gently heat butter, after it stops sizzling add the onions and soften on a low heat for 5 to 10 mins.
> ❖ Add the courgettes, mint leaves and stock, bring to the boil then simmer for 5 minutes.
> ❖ Using a food processor, blend half the soup until smooth. Combine the blended and unblended soup together, swirl in the cream and serve.

10 Potato Cakes

Potato cakes can be known by several other names: potato bread, potato scones or even potato scollops, which can lead to some confusion. Here in England, potato cakes are usually made from mashed potato and flour.

This version is using sweet potato, which automatically reduces the GI of this recipe. They are delicious served hot with a knob of butter or work equally well with a full English breakfast or a bowl of soup.

> ### Health Bite
>
> *Sweet potatoes provide some protein, vitamins C and E and huge amounts of carotenoids, including beta-carotene, which is beneficial for vision problems and cancer protection.*

Ingredients

Makes 6 potato cakes

- ➤ 1 medium sweet potato, peeled, cooked and mashed
- ➤ 1 ½ cups wheat-free bread flour (plus extra for dusting)
- ➤ salt and pepper
- ➤ butter or lard for cooking

Instructions

- ❖ In a bowl mix together the mashed potato and flour, and season well.
- ❖ Divide mixture into 6 balls.
- ❖ Roll each ball lightly in wheat-free flour and flatten down into disc shapes.
- ❖ Heat butter or lard in a large frying pan and add in the potato cakes, starting at the top and working around clock-wise.
- ❖ Cook for 2 to 3 minutes either side. Checking underneath each cake, if browning it's ready to turn, if not leave another minute and check again.
- ❖ Serve immediately.

11 Spicy Parsnip Soup

This soup is wonderful for lunch or dinner on a cold winter's day. It is surprisingly filling and nutritious.

> *Health Bite*
>
> *Parsnips are a good source of fiber, potassium, folic acid, vitamin E and have traces of minerals and B vitamins. They are a good remedy for fatigue and constipation.*

Ingredients

Serves 2 (double up ingredients for more servings)

- ➢ 2 medium parsnips, peeled and chopped
- ➢ 1 medium leek, trimmed and sliced
- ➢ 2 tsp ground cumin
- ➢ 2 tsp ground coriander
- ➢ 2 tsp stock or 1 stock pot (wheat or gluten-free)
- ➢ 2 tbsp. cream cheese
- ➢ ½ pint boiling water
- ➢ 1 tbsp. cold pressed coconut oil
- ➢ salt and pepper

Instructions

- ❖ Put the kettle on, half filled.
- ❖ Heat oil in a medium pan and soften the leeks for a few minutes, then add parsnips, cumin,

coriander, stock and pour in the boiling water, it should just cover the veg. Don't add too much water or your soup will have less flavor.

❖ Bring to the boil then simmer for 20 minutes.
❖ Take from heat, add cream cheese and blend till smooth. If too thick add a drop more boiling water.
❖ Season well and serve.

12 Waldorf Salad

This salad will brighten up the darkest days. It is light and refreshing and works well as a starter or light lunch.

> *Health Bite*
>
> *An apple a day keeps the doctor away! Apples are high in potassium and vitamin C, rich in plant compounds and the pectin content makes them a great form of soluble fiber.*

Ingredients

Serves 1 to 2

- ➢ handful of pecan or walnuts
- ➢ 1 dessert apple peeled and chopped
- ➢ juice of 1 lemon (to cover peeled apple to stop it from browning)
- ➢ 1 celery stick, peeled and chopped
- ➢ a few grapes, halved
- ➢ ½ a cup of natural organic yogurt
- ➢ handful of lettuce (rocket or other)
- ➢ salt and pepper to taste

Instructions

- ❖ Put peeled apple in a bowl with lemon juice.
- ❖ Lightly toast nuts in a frying pan for a few minutes then tip into bowl with apple.

❖ Add celery, grapes, lettuce and toss together.
❖ Pour over natural yogurt combine ingredients and season with salt and pepper, then serve.

13 Pea and Mint Soup

This soup is delicious whatever season you chose to make it. It is great as a starter, main meal or a filling lunch.

> **Health Bite**
>
> *Peas are packed with vitamins including C for heart health, K for bone protection and folate which helps prevent strokes.*

Ingredients

- 1 medium onion, diced
- 2 garlic cloves crushed or finely chopped
- good handful of mint leaves finely chopped
- 1 ½ pints of hot gluten-free stock (chicken or veg)
- 500g frozen peas (petit pois, garden or other)
- unrefined sea salt and ground black pepper
- double or single cream
- large knob of butter

Instructions

- Gently heat butter, after it stops sizzling add the onions and soften on a low heat for 5 to 10 mins.
- Add the peas, garlic, mint leaves and stock, bring to the boil then simmer for 5 minutes.
- Using a food processor blend the soup until smooth swirl in the cream and serve.

14 Greek Salad

This super-simple yet delicious salad can be enjoyed in the summer or winter months. It will brighten up any plate and is packed with nutrients.

Health Bite

Olives are one of the richest sources of monounsaturated fats. They are high in vitamin E, which is a powerful antioxidant, and are anti-inflammatory.

Ingredients

Serves 1 to 2

- ¼ of a cucumber diced (peeled is optional)
- 4 vine-ripened tomatoes, diced
- 6 green or black olives stoned and halved
- ¼ pack of feta cheese, cubed
- Extra virgin olive oil

Instructions

- ❖ Simply toss all the ingredients together, drizzle over virgin olive oil. Add salt and pepper to taste.

Dinner

1. Sweet chili salmon 165
2. Roast aubergines 166
3. Blue cheese cannelloni 168
4. Seafood and dill omelet 170
5. Kiev-style chicken 172
6. Tuna Madras 174
7. Sweet potato frittata 176
8. Veggie-potato hash 178
9. Veggie-sausages 180
10. Cauliflower cheese dumplings 182
11. Hearty pea soup 184
12. Chicken and tomato skewers 186
13. Grilled balsamic peppers 188
14. Spicy pork burgers 190
15. Pork moussaka 192
16. Lentil casserole 194
17. Courgette Pasta 196
18. Chickpea and coriander fritters 198
19. Pizza 200
20. Bangers and mash with onion gravy 202
21. Simple sole 204
22. Posh stilton mushrooms 205

1 Sweet Chili Salmon

Salmon is simple to cook and is incredibly versatile. It works well in light summer dishes or heartier winter dinners.

Health Bite

Being high in protein and omega 3 oils salmon is a superfood that nourishes the body and brain.

Ingredients

- 2 filets of salmon
- 2 tbsp. honey
- ½ tsp chili flakes
- 1 tbsp. gluten-free soya sauce

Instructions

- Mix together soy sauce, honey and chili flakes.
- Place salmon filets on a piece of foil, large enough to wrap into a parcel, pour honey-mix over salmon and wrap foil around.
- Place in a steamer or a preheated oven and cook for 15 to 25 minutes, depending on how well you like it cooked.

2 Stuffed Roasted Aubergines

Aubergines (eggplant) are very versatile. They can be used instead of pasta in lasagna, made into dips and are vegetarian friendly. As it uses both a grain and a pulse, this dish is a complete vegetarian protein.

> *Health Bite*
>
> *Aubergines are high in fiber and are packed with an array of nutrients such as vitamins and minerals: A, C, and folic acid, iron, calcium, magnesium and potassium.*

Ingredients

serves 4 as a starter, 2 as a main

> ➢ 4 oz. of brown rice or buckwheat
> ➢ 1 tsp of gluten-free stock (or a cube)
> ➢ 2 medium aubergines
> ➢ 6 spring onions, trimmed and finely sliced
> ➢ 4 tbsp. chopped coriander leaves
> ➢ 4 vine ripened tomatoes, finely chopped
> ➢ 1 14 oz. can of drained, rinsed, chickpeas
> ➢ 1 tsp ground cinnamon
> ➢ 2 tbsp. olive oil
> ➢ salt and pepper

Instructions

❖ Cook rice or buckwheat according to packet instructions with stock.
❖ Half the aubergines and carefully scoop out the flesh with a spoon.
❖ Finely chop the scooped-out flesh and mix with the rice or buckwheat and the rest of the ingredients, season and fill the aubergine skins with the mix.
❖ Pop the filled aubergines on a non-stick tray, cover with foil and bake for 25 minutes. Remove foil and cook for a further 15, or until the aubergines have collapsed.
❖ Serve immediately.

3 Blue Cheese Cannelloni

These cannelloni are made without any flour, making this a low GI dish. It is suitable for vegetarians yet by adding grilled chicken to either the tomato sauce or the blue cheese filling, makes it more satisfying for those who like extra protein.

> *Health Bite*
>
> *Tomatoes are rich in the antioxidants beta-carotene and lycopene, as well as vitamins C and E. They are great for cancer protection, skin and fertility problems.*

Ingredients

Serves 2

- 1 portion tomato sauce (page 231)
- Handful of grated cheese (Cheddar or parmesan)
- 4 eggs
- Cold pressed coconut oil for frying
- salt and pepper
- 2 tbsp. mayonnaise (gluten-free)
- 2 tbsp. cream cheese (gluten-free)
- 2 tbsp. blue cheese (such as Roquefort or Stilton)

Instructions

- ❖ First of all, make up blue cheese filling. Simply put mayonnaise, blue cheese and cream cheese into a food processor and blend until smooth.
- ❖ Whisk eggs together in a measuring jug and add seasoning.
- ❖ Heat oil in a small frying pan. Gently pour a small amount of mixture (remember this has to make 4 pancakes) into the hot pan and move pan around so mixture is evenly spread. When underneath is firm, gently flip omelet-pancake over and cook the other side. Repeat this with rest of mixture, making 4 pancakes.
- ❖ Take each pancake and spread generously with the blue cheese filling. Roll up and using a sharp knife or pizza cutter slice in half.
- ❖ Place 4 halves into 2 small, ovenproof dishes and top with tomato sauce and a sprinkling of cheese.
- ❖ Place in a preheated oven for 10 to 15 minutes or until bubbling.
- ❖ Serve immediately

4 Seafood and Dill Omelet

Taking omelets to another level! If you like seafood and eggs, then this dish is for you! It can be whipped up in minutes and makes a satisfying lunch or dinner.

> *Health Bite*
>
> *Eggs are an amazing source of protein and are little nutritional powerhouses. They are a rich source of zinc, vitamins A, D, E and the B vitamins, especially B12.*

Ingredients

Serves 2

- ➢ 6 to 8 oz. of cooked mixed seafood (or just prawns)
- ➢ juice of half a lemon
- ➢ 2 spring onions, trimmed and finely chopped
- ➢ 3 large eggs
- ➢ 2 tbsp. double cream
- ➢ 2 tbsp. dill chopped finely
- ➢ salt and pepper
- ➢ 1 tbsp. coconut oil and a knob of butter to fry

Instructions

- ❖ Place the seafood in a bowl with lemon juice and spring onions. Season and mix well.
- ❖ Place the eggs, dill and double cream in a bowl and beat together, then pour in seafood mix.

❖ Heat oil and butter in frying pan. After it stops sizzling pour in the egg mixture and coat the base of the pan evenly. Cook on a low heat for 10 minutes or until base is golden and all egg is set. Pop the omelet under a hot grill, for a couple of minutes, to brown the top.
❖ Serve immediately.

5 Kiev-Style Stuffed Chicken

This wheat, grain and gluten-free version of chicken Kiev is simple to make. The contrast of the textures and flavors make it a light yet satisfying dish.

> *Health Bite*
>
> *Organic chicken is a quality source of protein which helps maintain muscle mass. It contains all 9 required amino acids and is rich in potassium, essential for functioning of the body's cells and nervous tissues. It is also rich in the mood balancing mineral: selenium.*

Ingredients

- ➤ 2 large chicken breasts, skinned
- ➤ 4 oz. cream cheese
- ➤ 2 cloves of garlic, peeled and minced
- ➤ ½ tbsp. of finely chopped tarragon
- ➤ 1 tsp finely grated lemon zest
- ➤ 1 small courgette, thinly sliced
- ➤ salt and pepper
- ➤ 1 tbsp. olive oil

Instructions

- ❖ Sandwich each chicken breast between 2 pieces of cling film, triple the size of the chicken. Using a rolling pin or wooden mallet, gently beat chicken until it is double in size, being careful not to break the flesh.

❖ Preheat oven to 200ºC and line a baking tray with non-stick parchment.

❖ Mix together cream cheese, garlic, tarragon and lemon zest. Season well to taste. If mixture seems a little thick, add a drop of olive oil to loosen it.

❖ Lay the chicken on baking tray. Spread the cream cheese mixture on the chicken and place sliced courgettes on top of both pieces, neatly. Fold chicken in half to make an even sandwich, and using cocktail sticks, skewer chicken together. Season well and drizzle olive oil over.

❖ Place in oven and cook for 30 minutes or until chicken is cooked through and the filling is oozing.

❖ Serve immediately.

6 Tuna Madras

Although tinned tuna is not something you may associate as having in a curry, it goes surprisingly well. Tuna Madras is both easy and economical to make.

> Health Bite
>
> Tomatoes have a wide range of nutrients that protect us against disease. Onions contain flavonoids which help retain and build collagen in the skin.

Ingredients

Serves 4

- ➢ 1 large onion, peeled and diced
- ➢ 3 to 5 cloves of garlic, peeled and crushed
- ➢ 14 oz. of passata or tinned tomatoes
- ➢ 1 tsp Thai green curry paste
- ➢ 2 tbsp. Madras curry powder (wheat or gluten-free)
- ➢ 2 tsp honey or granulated stevia
- ➢ 1/4 cup dried coconut (optional)
- ➢ 1 small can of coconut milk (optional)
- ➢ 2 150g tins of tuna (1 tin per 2 persons) in oil or brine
- ➢ 2 tbsp. cold pressed coconut oil

Instructions

❖ Heat coconut oil and soften onions for 5 to 10 minutes.
❖ Next, add all ingredients except the coconut milk (if using) and tuna. Stir well, bring to the boil, then simmer on a low heat for 30 minutes. Stir often.
❖ Take from the heat and add coconut milk. Add the tuna, stir in and gently reheat.
❖ Serve with brown rice.

7 Sweet Potato Frittata

Frittata, which translates to 'fried' in Italian, is known as a classic egg-based brunch dish, similar to an omelet, crustless quiche or Spanish tortilla. What sets them apart is the way they are cooked.

Frittatas are normally cooked in a cast iron pan, stove-top, and are then finished in the oven (we'll be finishing ours under the grill).

Not only are they delicious but frittatas are quick and easy to prepare. They are protein-rich and, although known as a brunch dish, can be enjoyed for breakfast, lunch or dinner.

> *Health Bite*
>
> *Eggs are nutrient powerhouses that work amazingly well in both sweet and savory dishes and are perfect for anyone wanting to lose weight.*

Ingredients

Serves 4

- 12 oz. sweet potato, peeled, chopped and cooked
- 2 tbsp. lard, butter or coconut oil for cooking
- 1 large onion, diced
- 1 red pepper, deseeded and sliced
- 4 oz. frozen peas
- 6 large eggs beaten
- salt and pepper

Instructions

- ❖ In a large frying pan, heat 1 tbsp. cooking oil and cook the onion and red pepper for 5 minutes, then add the cooked sweet potato and frozen peas and cook for another couple of minutes.
- ❖ Pour the vegetables into the beaten egg mixture and season.
- ❖ Heat remaining oil in the frying pan and pour in the eggs and vegetables back in
- ❖ Cook on a low heat for 15 to 20 minutes or until the frittata appears to be set. Meanwhile preheat the grill.
- ❖ Pop the pan under the grill for 5 to 10 minutes, until the frittata is golden on top.
- ❖ Serve hot or cold.

8 Veggie-Potato Hash

This is a nutritious and satisfying dish which is perfect for those long, dark winter evenings.

> *Health Bite*
>
> *Peas provide an excellent source of thiamin (one of the B vitamins). They are also rich in folic acid and supply useful amounts of vitamins A and C as well as protein.*

Ingredients

Serves 4

- ➤ 1 pack of quick-soak dried peas, soaked as per packet instructions
- ➤ 2 carrots, peeled and chopped finely
- ➤ 1 large onion, peeled and diced
- ➤ 2 sticks of celery, peeled and finely chopped
- ➤ 2 medium potatoes peeled and cubed
- ➤ 1/2 pack wheat-free soya of Quorn mince
- ➤ 2 to 3 tsp of stock (wheat or gluten-free)
- ➤ 2 bay leaves
- ➤ 2 tbsp. oil
- ➤ salt and pepper
- ➤ ½ pint boiling water

Instructions

❖ Pop kettle on, half full.
❖ Heat oil and soften onions for 5 minutes.
❖ Next add the rest of the ingredients, except the Quorn mince, and pour in boiling water to just cover the veg and peas. Bring to the boil then cover and simmer for 15 minutes.
❖ Now, add in the Quorn mince, bring back to the boil, cover and simmer for 15 minutes.
❖ Remove bay leaves, season well and serve.

Please note: Quorn mince contains gluten but not wheat.

9 Veggie Sausages with Tomato Sauce

For the vegetarian, it is difficult to get healthy protein dishes without them containing wheat or gluten. This recipe is easy to make and freezes well.

> *Health Bite*
>
> *Cannellini beans are a great source of both protein and carbohydrate and are low GI. They are rich in B vitamins, high in iron, potassium and zinc and other essential minerals.*

Ingredients

Serves 4

For the sauce

- 9fl oz. passata
- 1 tbsp. gluten-free balsamic vinegar
- 1 tbsp. gluten-free Worcestershire sauce
- 2 tsp honey
- salt and pepper

For the sausages

- 1 14oz. tin cannellini beans, drained
- 2 carrots peeled and grated

- ➢ 1 brown onion, peeled and finely diced
- ➢ 6 tbsp. finely chopped parsley
- ➢ 1 tsp mixed herbs
- ➢ a dash of Tabasco sauce
- ➢ salt and pepper
- ➢ coconut oil for frying

Instructions

- ❖ To make sausages, place all sausage ingredients into a food processor and pulse together to combine.
- ❖ Chill the mixture in the fridge for a few hours.
- ❖ When ready to cook: place all sauce ingredients into a pan and gently bring up to the boil then simmer for 15 minutes. Whilst it simmers cook the sausages.
- ❖ Take balls of sausage mixture and roll into sausage shapes.
- ❖ Heat oil in pan and fry sausages, on a low to medium heat for 10 to 15 minutes turning continuously.
- ❖ Plate up the sausages and serve with the sauce, and your choice of veg or rice.

10 Cauliflower Cheese Dumplings

Why not try these delicious cauli-cheese dumplings as an alternative to meat or fish? They are economical and easy to make, and can be enjoyed cold the following day as a tasty snack.

> Health Bite
>
> *Cauliflower is low-carb and high in fiber. It is high in potassium and vitamin C.*

Ingredients

- ➢ 1 small head of cauliflower, chopped into chunks
- ➢ 2 large eggs beaten
- ➢ 2 oz. strong cheese (Parmesan, strong Cheddar or blue) grated or crumbled
- ➢ 2 oz. soya flour
- ➢ salt and pepper to season
- ➢ butter, lard or coconut oil to fry

Instructions

- ❖ Boil or steam the cauliflower until medium-soft, then mash.
- ❖ Add eggs, cheese, flour, salt and pepper and mix together.
- ❖ Shape into walnut-sized balls.
- ❖ Bring large pot of salted water to boil, in small batches drop in dumplings, when they rise to the

top remove with a slotted spoon and shake off excess water.

❖ Heat butter or oil in a frying pan, and fry dumplings until brown on either side.

11 Hearty Pea Soup

This is a real winter warmer! Hearty and satisfying...

Health Bite

Peas are an excellent source of thiamin (one of the B vitamins). They are also rich in folic acid and supply useful amounts of vitamins A and C as well as protein

---

Ingredients

Serves 4

- 1 pack of quick-soak dried peas, soaked as per packet instructions
- 2 carrots, peeled and chopped finely
- 1 large onion, peeled and diced
- 2 sticks of celery, peeled and finely chopped
- 2 to 3 tsp of stock (wheat or gluten-free)
- 2 bay leaves
- 2 tbsp. oil
- salt and pepper
- ½ pint boiling water

Instructions

- Pop kettle on, half full.
- Heat oil in a medium/large pan and soften onions for 5 to 10 minutes.

❖ Next add the rest of the ingredients to the pan and pour over boiling water, just enough to cover the veg and peas. Bring to the boil, cover and simmer for 20 minutes.
❖ Remove bay leaves and blend the soup, leaving some chunky veg pieces.
❖ Season well and serve.

12 Chicken and Tomato Skewers

This is a great one for the barbi! The longer the chicken is marinated the deeper the flavors become.

> *Health Bite*
>
> *Free range organic chicken contains many nutrients, including selenium which is great for improving moods.*

Ingredients

- ➢ 2 large chicken breasts chopped into bite-sized chunks
- ➢ 1 tbsp. medium curry powder
- ➢ 3 oz. natural yogurt
- ➢ juice of 1 lime
- ➢ 1/2 tbsp. unrefined sugar or honey
- ➢ 1 tsp cumin seeds
- ➢ 6 oz. cherry tomatoes

Instructions

- ❖ Mix the curry powder, yogurt, lime juice, sugar and cumin seeds into a glass bowl, then pop the chicken in and make sure all is well covered.
- ❖ Cover and marinate in a fridge for 6 to 8 hours or longer.
- ❖ Thread the chicken, alternating with the cherry tomatoes, onto 4 skewers.

❖ Cook in the oven for 12 to 15 mins, under the grill or on the barbi (turning often). Check chicken is cooked through before seasoning and serving.

13 Grilled Balsamic Peppers

The sweetness of the grilled peppers and the tang of the balsamic vinegar is a wonderful taste experience for the palate. Serve with brown rice.

> Health Bite
>
> Peppers are an excellent source of beta-carotene and vitamin C; they are also rich in calcium, phosphorus, sodium and potassium.

Ingredients

- 2 yellow peppers, halved and deseeded
- 2 red peppers, halved and deseeded
- 1 orange pepper, halved and deseeded
- 1 garlic clove, peeled and minced
- 2 tbsp. gluten-free balsamic vinegar
- unrefined sea salt and fresh ground black pepper
- handful of basil leaves
- 1 tbsp. olive oil

Instructions

- ❖ Place peppers on a foil-lined grill plate, insides down and place under a medium preheated grill for 15 minutes or until skins are charred. Remove from grill and place in a freezer bag and set aside for 10 minutes.

❖ When cool, peel off the pepper skins over a bowl to catch juices, then discard the skins. Slice the peppers into strips and add to bowl with olive oil, minced garlic and balsamic vinegar. Leave to marinate at room temperature for 30 minutes.
❖ When ready toss in basil leaves to serve.

14 Spicy Pork Burgers

These are so simple to make and go well with a delicious salad or a rice dish.

> **Health Bite**
>
> *Pork is an excellent source of protein but, unlike some other meats, cannot be eaten rare or even slightly uncooked.*

Ingredients

- 4oz. fine green beans blanched for 2 to 3 minutes chopped to 1"
- 1 brown onion, peeled and very finely diced
- 1lb 9oz. pork mince
- 1 tbsp. hot curry powder (such as Madras)
- 1/4 tsp unrefined sea salt
- cold pressed coconut oil for frying

Instructions

- In a bowel place all the ingredients, except the oil, and with your hands combine the mixture evenly.
- Cover and chill for a couple of hours
- When ready to cook, divide mixture into eight portions and fashion into burger shapes (not too thick to ensure cooked through thoroughly).
- Heat the oil in a large frying pan and add burgers, rotating burgers around the pan starting at 12 o'clock and finishing at 8 o'clock. This helps in knowing which burger to flip first.

❖ Cook burgers for 7 to 10 minutes each side. Cut open to ensure cooked, then serve.

15 Pork Mince Moussaka

Greek moussaka is typically made using lamb mince, however this version, using pork mince, works equally well. The only accompaniment needed with this dish is a simple salad.

> *Health Bite*
>
> *In addition to containing a host of vitamins and minerals, aubergines (also known as eggplant) contain phytonutrients which have antioxidant activity. They are a good source of dietary fiber, vitamin B1, and copper, as well as manganese, vitamin B6, niacin, potassium, folate, and vitamin K.*

Ingredients

Serves 2

- ➤ 1 medium-large aubergine (eggplant), cut into 1 cm thick slices
- ➤ 250g pork mince
- ➤ 1 medium onion, diced
- ➤ 3 cloves of garlic, minced
- ➤ 500g passata or tinned tomatoes
- ➤ 4 medium-sized mushrooms, chopped
- ➤ 3 tsp dark unrefined sugar
- ➤ ½ tbsp. wheat-free Worcestershire sauce
- ➤ ¼ tsp paprika
- ➤ ¼ tsp sea salt
- ➤ ¼ cup double cream
- ➤ 1 ball mozzarella, sliced into 1cm thick slices

- ➢ 1 oz. blue cheese (optional)
- ➢ 1 tbsp. butter

Instructions

- ❖ Heat butter in a pan, after it stops sizzling add in the chopped onion and cook for a couple of minutes before adding chopped mushrooms and cook on a low heat for 5 minutes.
- ❖ Add the minced garlic and pork mince and toss around with onions and mushrooms until mince is browned.
- ❖ Add passata (or tinned tomatoes), sugar, Worcestershire sauce, paprika and salt, bring to boil then simmer for 5 minutes.
- ❖ Meanwhile preheat oven at 180 to 200°C.
- ❖ In a medium baking dish place a layer of aubergine and pour over half the mince mixture, add another layer of aubergine, then pour over the rest of mince mixture.
- ❖ Lightly pour the double cream over the last layer of mince and top with the slices of mozzarella and, if using, blue cheese.
- ❖ Bake for 40 minutes, turn off the oven and leave to stand inside for another 10 minutes.
- ❖ Serve.

16 Lentil Casserole

This is a light yet filling dinner option that is easy on the purse strings. It is a simple one pot recipe which can be prepared in advance and heated in batches. Making it a great option for solo diners.

> *Health Bite*
>
> *Lentils are generally high in B vitamins, which are fantastic for improving the mood and are a good source of minerals, especially zinc.*

Ingredients

- ➢ 10 cloves
- ➢ 1 large onion peeled
- ➢ 225g Puy or green lentils
- ➢ 1 bay leaf
- ➢ 1.5 liters wheat-free vegetable stock
- ➢ 2 leeks sliced
- ➢ 2 sweet potatoes, peeled and diced
- ➢ 1 potato, peeled and diced
- ➢ 2 carrots, peeled and chopped
- ➢ 1 celery stick, peeled and chopped
- ➢ 1 tsp lemon juice
- ➢ 1 tbsp. olive oil
- ➢ salt and pepper

Instructions

- ❖ Preheat the oven.
- ❖ Press the cloves into the onion.

- ❖ Place the lentils into a large casserole dish with the bay leaf, onion and stock, cover and pop into the preheated oven for an hour.
- ❖ Remove onion, discard the cloves then chop the onion and return it to the dish with the rest of ingredients other than lemon juice. Mix together well before covering and returning to oven for 1 hour or until all vegetables are cooked and flavors infused.
- ❖ Remove bay leaf, stir in lemon juice and serve.

17 Courgette Pasta

Courgette pasta is super-simple to make and its delicate flavor will not overpower other flavors. You will need a spiralizer to make this dish. You can also make the pasta with sweet potato or any type of squash.

> *Health Bite*
>
> *Courgettes (zucchini) are great for the skin and are rich in Vitamin A. One serving provides a quarter of our daily needs of folic acid and is a rich source of potassium.*

Ingredients

Serves 2

- ➢ 2 medium courgettes
- ➢ 2 tbsp. butter
- ➢ 2 tbsp. grated parmesan
- ➢ 3 tbsp. double cream
- ➢ 1 cup of either cooked ham chopped or cooked salmon pieces (omit to make it vegetarian)

Instructions

- ❖ Use a spiralizer to make the courgette pasta.
- ❖ Heat the butter in large frying pan, just after it stops hissing, add the courgette spirals and toss around for a few minutes until slightly softened.

196

❖ Add the double cream, salmon or bacon and parmesan, then gently cook for a few more minutes.
❖ Serve immediately.

18 Chickpea and Coriander Fritters

Perfect for a light vegetarian supper these fritters are a nutritious, low cost source of protein for those who prefer not to eat meat.

This recipe can be also used with peas. Simply omit the coriander and chickpeas and instead add 300g defrosted frozen peas.

> *Health Bite*
>
> *Chickpeas are a great source of dietary fiber, which helps slow down the absorption rate of foods. This fiber also aids in preventing disorders of the digestive tract.*

Ingredients

- ½ cup all-purpose gluten-free flour
- 1 egg
- ½ tsp baking powder
- ½ cup milk
- 2 tsp onion granules
- 400g can chickpeas drained and rinsed
- 4 tbsp. chopped fresh coriander
- salt and pepper
- butter, lard or coconut oil for frying

Instructions

- ❖ Using a hand mixer or blender, mix the egg, flour, salt and pepper, milk and onion granules into a batter.

198

- ❖ Stir in chickpeas and coriander.
- ❖ Heat the oil or butter in a large frying pan.
- ❖ Add tablespoons of the batter in batches and cook for five minutes either side.

19 Pizza

There is no reason not to have pizza when following a wheat-free lifestyle. These bases are delicious and filling, with one small pizza being more than satisfying. Top them how you would your favorite pizzas. They can be made in advance and frozen.

> *Health Bite*
>
> *This base is complete in that in includes protein, carbohydrate and fat. It is also rich in essential nutrients, whilst being low-carb, so won't spike blood sugars.*

Ingredients

for 3 to 4 small to medium bases

- ➤ 2 cups fine ground almonds
- ➤ 1 medium head of cauliflower, grated (or pulsed in a food processor)
- ➤ 1 cup hard cheese such as Cheddar or parmesan
- ➤ 2 eggs
- ➤ 2 tsp onion granules (optional)
- ➤ salt and pepper

Instructions

- ❖ Preheat oven and line two baking trays with greaseproof paper
- ❖ In a large bowl firstly mix together all the ingredients with a wooden spoon then use your hands to combine the mix into a dough.
- ❖ Divide dough into 3 to 4 portions. Take each portion and flatten onto the baking tray with your hands to about ½ inch thick bases.

- ❖ Bake in oven for 15 minutes. Add chosen pizza topping, and bake for another 10 to 15 minutes. You need a gentle hand when removing them from the greaseproof paper as they are not as firm as regular bases.

Topping Ideas

Cheese and Tomato: Spread a thin layer of tomato puree over the base, place slices of mozzarella on top and a fine sprinkling of Italian herbs.

Barbecue Chicken: Spread a generous layer of sugar-free barbecue sauce over the pizza base, sprinkle grated Cheddar on top then add small chunks of cooked chicken.

Ham and Pineapple: Spread a thin layer of tomato puree over the base, place slices of mozzarella on top. Add small pieces of cooked ham and chunks of pineapple.

20 Bangers and Mash with Onion Gravy

This version of bangers 'n' mash is perfect for those wanting to lose weight. It has a low GI factor because it uses pumpkin and celeriac, instead of white potatoes.

> ### Health Bite
>
> *Celeriac is rich in potassium, vitamin C and B9. It is high in fiber. Not only does this fiber help the movement of the bowels, but also aids nutrient absorption. Pumpkin is incredibly rich in vital antioxidants and vitamins. It contains vitamin A and flavonoid poly-phenolic antioxidants such as leutin, xanthin, and carotenes in abundance, which help keep the skin glowing and youthful.*

Ingredients

Serves 2 to 3 (double up ingredients if required)

- 1 cup pumpkin peeled, deseeded and diced
- 1 cup of celeriac peeled and diced
- 1 tbsp. single or double cream
- 1 tbsp. butter
- salt and pepper
- 4 to 6 gluten/wheat-free sausages

For the gravy

- ➢ ½ pint gluten-free stock (meat, chicken or vegetarian)
- ➢ 1 medium brown onion
- ➢ 2 tsp cornstarch or arrowroot mixed with cold water into a paste
- ➢ 1 tbsp. cooking oil (lard, butter or coconut oil)

Instructions

- ❖ Cook sausages according to instructions on packet
- ❖ Put pumpkin and celeriac in a pan, bring to boil and simmer for 20 minutes or until soft.
- ❖ Whilst the vegetables and sausages are cooking make the gravy:
- ❖ Heat oil in pan, add onions, turn heat down and soften for 10 minutes. Add stock then bring back to boil, add arrowroot or cornstarch, reduce heat and simmer for 5 minutes.
- ❖ Drain pumpkin and celeriac, add cream and butter then mash or cream with hand blender. Add salt and pepper to taste.
- ❖ Divide mash between 2 to 3 plates, pile sausages on top, pour gravy over, et voila!

21 Simple Parsley Sole

This is a simple, quick dish to make but it is delicious and super-healthy!

> *Health Bite*
>
> *Parsley is one of the most nutritious herbs there is and has long-since been used as a traditional herbal remedy. It is a strong antioxidant and a good source of vitamin K.*

Ingredients

Serves 2 to 4

- 2-4 Sole filets (or plaice), 1 per person
- fresh squeezed lemon juice
- salt and pepper
- 1 tsp dried tarragon
- 1 tbsp. fresh chopped parsley

Instructions

- Preheat oven to 180°C
- Oil a baking dish large enough to hold fish filets. Place the filets in the dish and rub them with lemon juice, season with salt and pepper and sprinkle them with tarragon.
- Pop in the oven and bake for 18 minutes or until fish is flakey.
- Remove from oven and sprinkle with the fresh parsley. Serve immediately.

22 Posh Stilton Mushrooms

These get their name because they are made with cream instead of milk. They are an utterly delicious way to enjoy mushrooms. Served with a portion of savory or jasmine rice makes for a perfect evening meal.

> *Health Bite*
>
> *Mushrooms contain more protein than any other vegetable and are a great source of B12, which is particularly beneficial to those who eat little or no meat. They are packed with minerals, especially selenium*

Ingredients

- ➢ 12-18 medium-to-large mushrooms, washed and chopped
- ➢ 1 tbsp. butter
- ➢ ½ cup double cream
- ➢ ¾ cup blue Stilton, crumbled
- ➢ salt and pepper

Instructions

- ❖ Heat the butter in a medium saucepan and add the mushrooms, stir them around to coat them in butter, turn the heat down, cover and simmer for 20 minutes.
- ❖ Add the Stilton, cream, salt and pepper and stir. Simmer for another 5 minutes, or until sauce is creamy. Serve immediately.

Bakery & Desserts

1. Almond flour bread   207
2. Fluffy flaxseed bread   208
3. Cumin scented flatbread   210
4. Super bread   212
5. Feta, sun dried tomato and chickpea bread   214
6. Lemon scones   216
7. Banana and chocolate mousse   218
8. Sticky toffee pudding   219
9. Pears and chocolate sauce   222
10. Pancakes   224
11. Chocolate and courgette muffins   226
12. Chocolate and banana muffins   228
13. Hazelnut cookies   230
14. Berry cookies   232
15. Chocolate mountain muffins   234
16. Simple chocolate sauce   236
17. Egg custard   237

1 Almond Flour Bread

This bread recipe calls for almond flour, not ground almonds or almond meal, to make a lighter bread. Almond flour is not as readily available as ground almonds (at least not here in the UK) but can easily be ordered online.

> *Health Bite*
>
> *Almonds are packed with vitamin E which is a powerful antioxidant. They are great for keeping hunger at bay and balancing blood sugars after eating.*

Ingredients

> ➢ 2 cups almond flour (not ground almonds or meal)
> ➢ 2 tablespoons coconut flour
> ➢ ¼ cup ground flaxseeds
> ➢ ¼ teaspoon sea salt
> ➢ ½ teaspoon baking powder
> ➢ 5 large eggs
> ➢ 1 tablespoon apple cider vinegar

Instructions

> ❖ Preheat the oven 220°C
> ❖ Place almond flour, coconut flour, flaxseed, salt, and baking powder into a food processor and pulse together (or use hands in a bowl).
> ❖ Pulse in eggs and vinegar, until combined.
> ❖ Transfer batter to a small greased bread pan.
> ❖ Bake for 30 minutes.
> ❖ Cool in the pan for 2 hours before slicing.

2 Fluffy Flaxseed Bread

Flaxseed makes fantastic light, fluffy bread that is perfect for sandwiches. Because there is no yeast in this recipe, the rise comes from the baking powder and the eggs. It can be frozen but is best to slice the bread first.

> *Health Bite:*
>
> *Flaxseeds, sometimes called linseed, are packed with nutrients. They are high in both soluble and insoluble fiber, perfect for good digestive health and contain the essential fatty acid, omega-3.*

Ingredients

- ➤ 1 ½ cup arrowroot powder
- ➤ 1 cup ground flaxseed
- ➤ 4 whole eggs
- ➤ 4 egg whites whisked till fluffy
- ➤ 4 tbsp. butter softened
- ➤ 1 ½ tsp rock or sea salt
- ➤ 4 tsp baking powder (gluten-free)
- ➤ 2 tsp apple cider vinegar
- ➤ coconut oil to grease bread pan

Instructions

- ❖ Preheat the oven 220 ºC.
- ❖ Rub the small bread loaf pan with the coconut oil.
- ❖ In a bowl, combine the arrowroot powder, flaxseed meal, baking powder and sea salt. Stir to incorporate.

- ❖ In a blender or separate bowl, combine 4 whole eggs, 4 egg whisked whites and blend until thoroughly mixed.
- ❖ Pour the egg mixture into the arrowroot and flaxseed and mix until there are no lumps.
- ❖ Pour into a small greased bread loaf pan. Bake uncovered for 30-35 minutes.
- ❖ Allow to cool before slicing and serving.

3 Cumin Scented Flatbread

These flatbreads are tasty, filling and very low GI. They are great for snacks, lunches or party treats and freeze well. Double up the ingredients and pop them in the freezer for a later date.

> *Health Bite*
>
> *Flaxseeds, sometimes called linseed, are packed with nutrients. They are high in both soluble and insoluble fiber, perfect for good digestive health and contain the essential fatty acid, omega-3.*

Ingredients

makes 6 flatbreads

- 1/2 cup warm water
- 1 1/2 tsp fast action yeast
- 1 cup almond meal (ground almonds)
- 1 cup gram flour (chickpea flour)
- 1/2 cup ground flaxseeds (linseed)
- 1 tsp salt
- 1 tsp dark unrefined sugar
- 1 tsp cumin seeds, lightly toasted
- 1 tbsp. olive oil in a small bowl

Instructions

- Preheat oven 200 ºC

- ❖ Dissolve yeast and sugar in the warm water and set aside for 10 minutes
- ❖ Mix the rest of the dry ingredients together in a bowl and sift well using hands and fingers.
- ❖ Pour yeast mixture in dry ingredients and mix well with a spoon. The bread mixture should be sticky, if dry add a drop more water.
- ❖ Line baking tray with greaseproof paper
- ❖ Coat palm of hands with a small amount of oil (to prevent mix from sticking to hands) and pick a small clump of mix, roll into a ball and flatten down into a flatbread shape then place onto baking tray. Do this again with the rest of mix, making 6 flatbreads.
- ❖ Place in oven and bake for 8 to 10 minutes.

Serving Suggestion:

Great with humus, tzatziki, sour cream and chive dip, or dipped into melted Camembert.

4 Super Bread

This hearty loaf is perfect for sandwiches, toasting, dipping, slathering in butter or eaten any way you prefer. It is very filling so you won't need more than 1 or 2 slices!

For a stronger flavored herb bread, add in a 1 tsp each of rosemary, oregano, onion granules and garlic powder

> *Health Bite*
>
> *This bread contains all the essential amino acids the body needs as well as the major minerals, it's a complete protein, high in fiber, both soluble and insoluble, rich in vitamin E and omega-3, as well as being low GI.*

Ingredients

Makes 1 small loaf, double ingredients for a larger loaf and add 10 mins to bake time

- ➢ 2 cups wheat/gluten-free bread flour
- ➢ 2 cups almond meal (ground almonds)
- ➢ 1 cup ground flaxseed (otherwise known as linseed)
- ➢ ½ tsp ground black pepper
- ➢ 1 tsp sea salt
- ➢ 2 tsp dark unrefined sugar
- ➢ 2 tbsp. natural yogurt
- ➢ 1 tsp Xanthan gum

- ➤ 2 tsp baking powder
- ➤ 1 ½ cups black tea (stew a tea bag in hot water as though making a cup of tea)
- ➤ 2 eggs

Instructions

- ❖ Preheat oven at 200 ºC
- ❖ Mix together all dry ingredients with fingers to ensure there's no lumps then add in eggs and black tea and combine well.
- ❖ Pour mixture into a small bread tin that has been lined with greased, greaseproof paper and bake for 25 to 30 minutes.
- ❖ Cool on a wire rack, slice and serve.

This bread freezes well (slice before freezing) and is great to use for breadcrumbs.

–

5 Feta, Sun dried Tomato and Chickpea Bread

Delicious and easy to make, this bread will brighten up many meals. It can be served as an appetizer with olive oil and balsamic vinegar, it goes well with soup and salad and even works with bacon and poached eggs.

> *Health Bite*
>
> *Sun dried tomatoes are high in several nutrients such as vitamin C and K, and minerals potassium, copper and manganese. They are also high in fiber, which is beneficial to the digestive tract, helps digestion and aids in elimination.*

Ingredients for Medium Loaf

- 2 cups chickpea flour (gram, garbanzo or besan flour)
- 2 cups plain gluten/wheat-free bread flour
- 1 cup fine grain polenta (maize)
- ¾ pint warm water
- 3 tsp unrefined sugar or honey
- 1 packet easy-yeast
- 4 pieces of sun-dried tomato, finely chopped
- 2 oz. feta cheese crumbled
- 2 tsp dried rosemary
- 2 tsp unrefined sea salt

Instructions

- ❖ Preheat oven to 200ºC.

- ❖ Dissolve the sugar and yeast in the water and stir well with a balloon whisk.
- ❖ Line a medium loaf tray with well-greased parchment.
- ❖ Place all dry ingredients together in a large bowl and thoroughly mix together with hands, ensuring all flours are well blended.
- ❖ Pour sugar, yeast and water into dry ingredients and mix well with a heavy spoon. Mixture should resemble a thick batter (not a dough).
- ❖ Pour batter into loaf tin and bake for 40 mins or until firm to touch.
- ❖ Remove from tin and cool on a wire rack.

6 Lemon Scones

These lemon scones are super scrummy and every bit as good as the wheat version. Being higher on the GI they should be enjoyed as an occasional treat or when guests are coming for afternoon tea. They don't tend to stay fresh long, even in an airtight container, so are best eaten within 24 hours of baking, but are well worth the effort (not to say there's much effort needed to make them).

Gluten-free baking can be very hit and miss. As in, after following a recipe to the letter, there is no guarantee of an exact result each time. There are many varying factors for this, the most common being oven and room temperature, before, during and after baking. Yet, this recipe seems to work the same each time.

Ingredients

Makes 12 scones

- ➤ 2 tsp lemon extract (this can be omitted to make plain scones)
- ➤ 2 ½ cups gluten-free flour (I use bread flour)
- ➤ ¼ to ½ cup xylitol, granulated stevia (depending on one's sweet tooth) or honey
- ➤ 1 ½ tsp gluten-free baking powder
- ➤ 1 medium egg
- ➤ 1 cup plain natural yogurt (full-fat)
- ➤ ½ cup milk (dairy or non-dairy)
- ➤ ½ cup softened butter (2 oz.)

Instructions

- ❖ Preheat oven to 200 °C.
- ❖ Grease medium muffin tins (or use non-stick).
- ❖ Place all ingredients into a large bowl, using a hand mixer, blend to a thick but smooth consistency, like a heavy cake batter. If it seems too thick add a drop more milk.
- ❖ Pour mixture into muffin cases and bake for 20 mins (or until risen and firm to touch).
- ❖ Cool on a wire rack.
- ❖ Serve on their own or with a generous layer of clotted cream.

7 Banana and Chocolate Mousse

If you've got a serious hankering for a chocolate-fix, this recipe will certainly hit the mark. It is incredibly indulgent, easy to whip up and, if you're following a low sugar/carb/GI plan, won't spike your blood sugar.

> *Health Bite*
>
> *Bananas are one of nature's miracle foods, being packed full of nutrients they are the ultimate fast food, which come in their own packaging!*

Ingredients

Serves 4

- 1 large ripe banana mashed
- 1 cup of double cream, whipped to thick consistency
- ½ cup cream cheese
- 1 ½ tbsp. cocoa powder
- 2 tsp granulated stevia (Truvia) or 1 tbsp. honey

Instructions

- Simply place all above ingredients into a medium bowl and mix together with a hand mixer.
- Check for sweetness of recipe. Depending on one's sweet tooth more sweetener may be required.
- Spoon mixture into ramekins and chill for 2 hours or until needed.

8 Sticky Toffee Pudding

This is one version of sticky toffee pudding where you will not miss wheat or gluten. It is easy to make, truly delicious and filling, so make sure you leave space for it after your meal!

Health Bite

Dried dates are nutritional powerhouses, they are packed with a range of vitamins and minerals beneficial to all areas of health, they are a good source of energy and their content of B5 (pantothenic acid) makes them perfect for maintaining or attaining luxuriously glossy hair and glowing skin.

Ingredients

Serves 4

- 1 cup of pitted dried dates, soaked in 2 cups boiling water for 20 minutes
- 1 cup almond meal
- 1 cup gram flour (chick pea)
- 1 egg
- 1 tsp baking powder
- ½ cup unrefined dark brown sugar
- 1/3 cup softened butter or coconut oil, plus extra for greasing

for the toffee sauce

- ➤ 2 tbsp. butter
- ➤ 4 tbsp. dark unrefined sugar
- ➤ 2 tbsp. double cream

Instructions

- ❖ Preheat oven 200ºC. Line a medium baking tin with greased, greaseproof paper.
- ❖ Using a hand blender or food processor, blend the soaked dates and soaking water together.
- ❖ Place dry ingredients: almond meal, gram flour, sugar and baking powder into a bowl and combine thoroughly.
- ❖ Next, add the rest of the ingredients: egg, butter or oil and blended dates, and mix together into a batter.
- ❖ Pour batter into a lined, medium-sized, square baking dish or tray, pop into oven and bake for 25 mins, or until firm to touch.
- ❖ Remove from oven and allow to cool in tray or dish whilst you make the sauce.
- ❖ Place butter and sugar into a small pan and gently heat (not too hot or butter will burn) until butter and sugar melt and combine into a sauce.
- ❖ Pour in cream, heat through and your sauce is ready to serve.
- ❖ Slice sticky toffee pudding, place into serving dishes, pour on toffee sauce and serve with sugar free ice cream or custard... delish!

This pudding can be made the day before being needed and reheated in microwave.

The toffee sauce is best made fresh on the day.

9 Pears and Chocolate Sauce

Pears are a beautiful dessert fruit and with the addition of chocolate sauce makes this pudding a scrumdiddlyumptious treat!

> *Health Bite*
>
> *Pears are high in soluble fiber making them great for easing constipation and soothing intestinal inflammations. They are also a useful source of iron, vitamins A and C and a little vitamin E.*

Ingredients

Serves 2

- ➢ 1 tsp lemon juice (to stop pears discoloring)
- ➢ 2 slightly under-ripe pears, peeled cored and halved, covered in lemon juice
- ➢ 1 tbsp. honey
- ➢ 1 ½ pints water

For the chocolate sauce:

- ➢ 1 cup of milk (coconut, almond or dairy)
- ➢ 50 grams of dark chocolate
- ➢ Splash of double cream (optional)

Instructions

- ❖ Bring the water to boil in a large sauté pan add honey and allow to dissolve.
- ❖ Add the pears and simmer for 15 to 20 minutes, partially covered, until tender.
- ❖ Whilst the pears are simmering, pour milk into small pan, break up chocolate and add to milk. Gently heat and stir until chocolate is melted and combined with milk. Add splash of double cream if desired.
- ❖ Remove pears from pan with a slotted spoon, place into serving bowls, pour over chocolate sauce and enjoy...

10 Pancakes

I love pancakes and this version is every bit as good as the wheat flour one, especially when slathered with a delicious topping. These are a bit of a treat and should only be enjoyed occasionally. It is a great recipe to have on hand if you have children in the house. They can be served as you like, but are particularly good as a dessert, with bananas and cream, or as part of a main meal with a creamy chicken and mushroom filling.

> **Health Bite:**
>
> *Eggs are mini nutrient powerhouses and amongst some of the most nutritious foods on the planet. They are an amazing source of protein and amino acids.*

Ingredients

Makes 6 small pancakes

- 1 egg
- 125g wheat-free plain flour
- 250ml milk (or half water, half milk)
- 1 tsp baking powder
- knob of butter or coconut oil for frying

Instructions

- Place the flour and baking powder into a mixing bowl.
- In a jug, whisk together egg and milk.
- Using an electric hand mixer (or balloon whisk), slowly pour egg and milk into flour and mix well.

As all flours are different the mix may need a little extra fluid. If the batter appears too thick, after egg and milk poured in, add a drop more milk until consistency is thinner.

❖ Heat butter in a small frying pan, just after it stops sizzling, pour in a small amount of batter and swirl around the pan to spread out (for smaller thicker pancakes don't swirl mixture around). Cook for a minute or two, then flip up edge to check it is browning underneath, if it looks dark golden, flip it over and cook the other side (if you try flipping it too soon the pancake will break up). Pop onto a plate.

❖ Continue this way with the rest of mixture. Stack pancakes on top of each other, and place under a warmed grill until ready to serve.

Note: to make thicker pancakes simply reduce the amount of milk in this recipe.

11 Chocolate and Courgette Muffins

Yes, I know this sounds like a hideous combination, yet these muffins are surprisingly delicious! For one thing the courgette is not recognizable as a vegetable in the muffin (great if your kids hate green veg, which they don't even need to know they're eating), and the flavor blends perfectly well with the coconut flour and chocolate. Also, the courgette gives the muffin an interesting texture.

> *Health Bite*
>
> *These muffins are grain-free, gluten-free low-carb, low GI, sugar-free, fiber-rich, filling and totally awesome!*

Ingredients for 6 large muffins

- ½ cup coconut flour
- 3 large eggs
- ½ cup granulated stevia (such as Truvia)
- 1 small courgette grated
- ¼ cup cocoa powder (may also add ¼ cup dark chocolate chopped into small pieces)
- ½ cup melted butter or coconut oil
- ½ tsp baking powder

Instructions

- ❖ Preheat oven at 200°C.
- ❖ Mix all above ingredients together in a large bowl with an electric whisk.
- ❖ If mix seems on thick side when whisked, add a drop of fluid such as milk, it should be like a thick batter.
- ❖ Pour mix into 6-hole, non-stick muffin tray and bake for 15 to 20 minutes.
- ❖ Allow to cool on a baking tray, then enjoy

12 Chocolate and Banana Muffins

A great way to include more fruit into your diet is to add it into your baking and cooking. Adding very ripe bananas to your cakes and muffins means the recipe will need less sweetener. It also increases the soluble fiber content.

These muffins are yummy eaten on their own, but become even more delicious when served with a generous serving of whipped cream and strawberries.

> ### Health Bite
>
> *As an aid to lifting mood, bananas are a must-have. They are a good source of the amino acids which convert into serotonin and dopamine; the body's natural feel good hormones, vital for keeping stable emotional balance.*

Ingredients

Makes 12 muffins

- ➤ 2 medium ripe bananas (browning), mashed
- ➤ 2 medium eggs
- ➤ ½ cup fine polenta
- ➤ 1 ½ cups gluten-free self-raising flour
- ➤ 3/4 cup xylitol or stevia
- ➤ 2 tbsp. cocoa powder, sifted
- ➤ 1 cup coconut oil or butter, melted
- ➤ 2 cups milk (dairy, almond or soya)
- ➤ 1 tsp gluten-free baking powder

Instructions

- ❖ Preheat oven at 180°C.
- ❖ Place all the ingredients into a bowl and using a hand blender, whisk up until mix is a smooth and fluffy consistency.
- ❖ Pour mix into greased muffin tins or cases and pop into preheated oven.
- ❖ Bake for 15 to 20 minutes until firm to touch.
- ❖ Cool on a wire rack.

Will keep for 3 days in an airtight container.

13 Hazelnut Cookies

In need of a sweet indulgent treat...? Crispy, crunchy and incredibly moreish, these cookies can be enjoyed at any time of the day and they certainly hit the mark!

> *Health Bite*
>
> *Hazelnuts are an excellent source of protein, fiber and magnesium. They also contain iron, zinc and lots of vitamin E.*

Ingredients

- ½ cup toasted, ground hazelnuts
- 1 cup ground almonds
- 1 cup brown rice flour
- 3 oz. butter
- ½ cup dark unrefined sugar

Instructions

Preheat oven to 220 ºC

- On a low heat melt sugar and butter together to combine.
- Combine all dry ingredients together in a bowel.
- Once butter and sugar combined, allow to cool a little before mixing all ingredients together into a dough.
- Line 2 trays with greaseproof paper. Take small clumps of dough, roll into a ball then flatten into a

disk and place on baking tray. Continue like this
with the rest of the dough, ensuring gaps are kept
between shortbread to allow them to spread.
* Pop into oven for 8 to 10 minutes, or until just
browning on the edges.
* Leave on baking trays for 10 minutes before
carefully (the shortbread are quite delicate and
crumbly) transferring to cooling rack.

14. Berry Cookies

These cookies are perfect for satisfying a sweet tooth whilst being super-healthy at the same time. They are great for a breakfast on the go or for the mid-afternoon-munchies! The recipe can be varied adding more or less of your preferred ingredients.

> Health Bite
>
> Dried fruit are an excellent source of instant energy, which are popular with athletes. They provide significant amounts of iron, potassium and selenium and are high in fiber. They make excellent substitutes for refined sugar in recipes.

Ingredients

Makes 8 to 18 cookies, depending on how large you make them

- ➢ 2 cups almond meal (ground almonds)
- ➢ ½ cup mixed dry berries (such as blackberry, blueberry, goji berry, acai berry)
- ➢ 1 large egg, beaten
- ➢ ½ cup dried, unsweetened, coconut
- ➢ ½ cup mixed seeds (sesame, sunflower, etc.)
- ➢ ¼ cup unrefined sugar or honey
- ➢ 1 tsp baking powder (gluten-free)
- ➢ 1 tsp vanilla essence
- ➢ 2 tbsp. oil (melted coconut, butter, rapeseed)

Instructions

- ❖ Preheat oven at 220 ºC
- ❖ Put all the dry ingredients together in a bowl (including sugar if not using honey) and mix together with hands ensuring there are no clumps.
- ❖ Add moist ingredients, egg, vanilla essence, oil and honey if using, and mix well.
- ❖ Line baking trays with greaseproof paper
- ❖ Take clumps of mix and roll into even-sized balls (depending on cookie size you prefer), flatten and place on baking trays, ensuring space between each one. **Tip:** *if the mix is very sticky coat the palm of your hands in oil beforehand.*
- ❖ Place in oven and bake for 8 to 10 mins.

Store in an airtight container for up to a week.

15 Chocolate Mountain Muffins

From the outside, there doesn't appear to be any chocolate in sight. However, one bite is all it takes to reveal the delicious, dark chocolate oozing out from the muffin (especially if eaten soon after baking). These are a real treat and although very moreish, they are also filling, so you don't need to worry about overindulging.

> *Health Bite*
>
> *The high almond and egg content of these muffins lowers their glycemic load, which prevents the sugar-rush and stops those hunger-pangs associated with eating wheat muffins.*

Ingredients

6 large or 12 small muffins

- ➢ 3/4 cup polenta
- ➢ 2 cups almond meal (ground almonds)
- ➢ ½ cup granulated stevia or xylitol
- ➢ 50g dark chocolate, chopped into small chunks (made from min 75% cocoa solids and unrefined sugar).
- ➢ 1 tsp baking powder
- ➢ 2 eggs
- ➢ ½ cup milk (dairy or non-dairy)
- ➢ ½ cup (2 oz.) melted butter

Instructions

- ❖ Heat oven at 220ºC and grease muffin tray/s
- ❖ Combine all the ingredients together in a bowl and mix well with a hand mixer
- ❖ Pour into muffin cases and pop in oven and bake for 20 minutes, or until firm to touch.
- ❖ Cool on a wire rack.

16 Simple Chocolate Sauce

This is a great pouring sauce which is delicious served with many of your favorite puddings. It can also be used as a chocolate fondue, for your favorite fruits, or if left to set in the fridge for a few hours, the sauce becomes a chocolate mousse.

Ingredients

Serves 1 to 2 as a mousse or 2 to 3 as a sauce.

- 1 cup of milk (coconut, almond or regular)
- 50 grams dark chocolate
- 1 tbsp. of double cream (optional)
- *(For chocolate orange flavor add the zest of 1 orange)*

Instructions

- Pour milk into small pan, break up chocolate and add to milk (if using orange zest add now). Gently heat and stir until chocolate is melted and combined with milk.
- If you want to make a thicker sauce or mousse, add the double cream.
- Serve immediately as a sauce or chill to thicken.

17 Egg Custard

This is a lovely light dessert that is scrumptious served with chopped banana.

> ### *Health Bite:*
>
> *Eggs are amongst some of the most nutritious foods on the planet. The yolks can even be eaten by those who have a sensitivity towards whole eggs.*

Ingredients

- ¾ cup milk
- 2 egg yolks, well beaten
- ½ tbsp. honey (or to taste)
- ½ tsp pure vanilla extract (sugar-free) or vanilla seeds

Instructions

Heat the milk to boiling pint, remove from heat and slowly add into the egg yolks, stirring continuously.

Pour all the mixture back into pan and return to a low heat, stirring until it thickens slightly.

Stir in vanilla extract and honey. The custard will thicken as it cools

Side Dishes, Bits & Bobs

1. Salad dressings   239
2. Sardine pâté   241
3. Creamy coleslaw   242
4. Wilted leafy greens   243
5. Pumpkin and celeriac mash   244
6. Yoghurt and mint dip   245
7. Sautéed carrot and courgette medley   246
8. Loaded potato skins   248
9. Creamed Brussel sprouts   250
10. Rosemary roast sweet potatoes   251
11. Tomato sauce   252
12. Stuffing   254
13. Bone broth   256

1 Salad Dressings

A great way of including lots of raw enzyme packed nutrients to your diet is by having a salad at least once a day with lunch or dinner.

When making dressings, I usually chuck all the ingredients into a blender and whizz them together. But if you don't own a blender or food processer, a clean screw-top jar works well. Pop the ingredients in jar, secure the lid and give it a really good shake. All dressings will keep in sealed container in fridge for up to a week.

Here are a few delicious dressings that will brighten up any plate.

Ranch Dressing

16 servings

- ➤ 1 cup soured cream
- ➤ ½ cup mayonnaise
- ➤ 1tbsp. white wine vinegar
- ➤ ¼ cup parmesan cheese grated
- ➤ 1 tsp garlic powder
- ➤ 1 ½ tsp onion powder
- ➤ Pinch salt

Instructions

- ❖ Place in a blender and whip up for 30 seconds

Thousand Island Dressing

16 servings

- ➤ ½ cup mayonnaise

- ➢ ½ cup soured cream
- ➢ ¼ cup sugar-free tomato ketchup
- ➢ ½ tsp paprika
- ➢ 1 tsp lemon juice

Instructions:

- ❖ Place in a blender and whip up for 30 seconds

Blue Cheese Dressing

8 servings

- ➢ 4 tbsp. soured cream
- ➢ 4 tbsp. buttermilk
- ➢ ¼ cup crumbled strong blue cheese
- ➢ 2 tbsp. Parmesan cheese, grated
- ➢ 1 tsp onion powder

Instructions:

- ❖ Place in a blender and whip up for 30 seconds

2 Sardine Pâté

Sardine pâté can be whipped up in minutes. It is tasty and a great alternative to tuna or salmon pâté. Sardines are also a fabulous low-cost source of protein.

> *Health Bite*
>
> *Sardines are packed with 2 omega-3 fatty acids, DHA and EPA. They are one of the few foods rich in vitamin D, which is essential for bone health and helps prevent Seasonal Affected Disorder (SAD).*

Ingredients

- ➢ 2 x 120g cans of sardines in oil
- ➢ 250g full-fat cream cheese
- ➢ 2 tbsp. capers
- ➢ 6 tbsp. finely chopped parsley
- ➢ squeeze of lemon (optional)
- ➢ salt and pepper to taste

Instructions

- ❖ Place all the ingredients into a food processor and blend until smooth.
- ❖ Put mixture into a serving bowl and chill until needed.

3 Creamy Coleslaw

Coleslaw is a great comfort food. It goes well with meat, fish, poultry and vegetarian dishes. The delicate, sweet flavor of the carrots is a perfect accompaniment to the pungency of the cabbage and onion.

> *Health Bite*
>
> *Carrots are a super-food which contain vitamins B, C, D, E, K, folic acid and beta-carotene and are excellent for supporting and strengthening the immune system.*

Ingredients

- 1 large carrot peeled and grated
- ¼ of a head of cabbage (red or green) shredded finely
- ¼ onion finely diced
- 2 tbsp. of gluten-free mayonnaise or use 1 tbsp. natural yogurt, 1 tbsp. mayonnaise
- salt and pepper to taste

Instructions

- In a bowl mix all ingredients together, add required salt and pepper.
- Serve or cover and chill. Will keep for 2 days in the fridge.

4 Wilted Leafy Greens

Being so important to our health, we all need to include darker leafy veg into our diet and this recipe is a great way of doing just that. It is super quick and ready in minutes, and goes well with any meat, fish or vegetarian recipe.

> *Health Bite*
>
> *Kale is one of the most nutritious green vegetables there is. It tops the chart for calcium content and has as many as 45 different antioxidant compounds which are essential for keeping a healthy immune system.*

Ingredients

- ➢ 2 cups kale, stems removed
- ➢ 1 cup spinach
- ➢ 2 cups spring greens
- ➢ 2 tbsp. olive oil
- ➢ ½ cup water
- ➢ salt and pepper

Instructions

- ❖ Rip the greens into small pieces.
- ❖ Heat a large saucepan and add the water, oil and kale. Cover and let the kale wilt for 1 minute.
- ❖ Add the spring greens and wilt for a minute before adding the spinach for another minute or two.
- ❖ Drain excess water and season. Serve immediately.

5 Pumpkin and Celeriac Mash

As an alternative to mashed potato, why not try this low GI, super healthy tasty version?

Health Bite

Celeriac is rich in potassium, vitamin C and B9. It is high in fiber and not only does this fiber help the movement of the bowels but also the nutrient absorption.

Ingredients

- 1 cup pumpkin peeled, deseeded and diced
- 1 cup of celeriac, peeled and diced
- 1 tbsp. single or double cream
- 1 tbsp. butter
- salt and pepper

Instructions

- Place pumpkin and celeriac in a pan and bring to the boil, then simmer for 20 minutes or until veg are tender.
- Drain pumpkin and celeriac, add cream and butter then mash or cream with hand mixer.
- Add salt and pepper to taste.

6 Yogurt and Mint Dip

Light and refreshing this dip is a great accompaniment for veggie-burgers or kebabs.

> *Health Bite*
>
> *Authentic Greek yogurt is a great source of protein and is rich in probiotics which is beneficial to the intestinal flora.*

Ingredients

- ➤ 1 cup of full-fat Greek Yogurt
- ➤ 1 tbsp. fresh mint, very finely chopped
- ➤ 1 tsp honey
- ➤ pinch of salt if desired

Instructions

- ❖ Put all ingredients into a bowl and, using a hand blender, whisk together.
- ❖ Pour into serving bowl or chill until needed.

7 Sautéed Carrot and Courgette Medley

We get most nutrients from veg in their raw state, however, when raw they tend to be harder for the body to digest, hence the need to cook. To retain as many nutrients as possible, it is best to cook veg for just a short time and this is where sautéing comes in.

> *Health Bite*
>
> *Not only are carrots delicious but highly nutritious too. They are rich in carotene and antioxidants, believed to improve concentration and memory, help protect against cancer, heart disease and eye problems.*

Ingredients

Serves 2

- ➢ 2 medium carrots peeled, topped and tailed
- ➢ 1 medium courgette
- ➢ large knob of butter or coconut oil
- ➢ 1 tbsp. fresh mixed herbs, chopped finely (optional) such as thyme, sage and parsley
- ➢ salt and pepper

Instructions

- ❖ Using a vegetable peeler, finely slice the carrot and courgettes into long slithers or use a spiralizer.

- ❖ Using a sauté or frying pan, melt the butter or oil. and add the veg and herbs, if using, and season well.
- ❖ Lightly toss the veg around in pan for 3 to 5 minutes, till lightly softened.
- ❖ Serve immediately

8 Loaded Potato Skins

As this dish is using the skins of the potatoes and not the flesh, it lowers the GI and makes the nutritional value greater. Save the flesh of potatoes, mash then either freeze or store in fridge for a few days, and use when making fish cakes or veggie-burgers.

> *Health Bite*
>
> *Sweet potatoes are packed with vitamin A and are a good source of beta-carotene. They are a much more nutritious choice of starchy carbohydrate and contain vitamin E, which is beneficial to dry skin conditions.*

Ingredients

Serves 2 to 4

- ➢ 2 sweet potatoes
- ➢ 2 brown potatoes
- ➢ 1/2 tbsp. oil (such as rapeseed or olive)
- ➢ 1 cup of good grated cheese (your preference here but one that's good for melting)
- ➢ unrefined sea salt

For the dip:

- ➢ ½ cup authentic full-fat Greek yogurt
- ➢ ¼ cup full-fat mayonnaise

- ➢ 1 large of clove garlic
- ➢ salt and pepper to taste

Instructions

- ❖ Preheat oven to 220°C.
- ❖ Prick the potatoes lightly, rub oil into the skins and sprinkle with sea salt. Put brown potatoes in the oven for 15 minutes then add the sweet potatoes for a further 40 minutes or until soft. Don't allow sweet potatoes to overcook as they become mushy.
- ❖ Whilst potatoes are baking make the dip. Combine all dip ingredients into a food processor and blend till smooth. Transfer to a serving bowl and chill till needed.
- ❖ When potatoes are cooked, halve them and scoop out flesh with a spoon (please note: sweet potato skins will be softer and you will need to retain more flesh to keep them firm). Then halve the skins again. Sprinkle cheese over and put back in oven for another 5 minutes to melt cheese.
- ❖ Serve immediately with a teaspoon of dip on each skin.

9 Creamed Brussel Sprouts

This is an alternative way to cook sprouts and can be enjoyed by those who wouldn't normally eat them.

> *Health Bite*
>
> *Brussel sprouts have the same health benefits as other members of the brassica family. They are a good source of vitamin C and beta-carotene and are beneficial for all skin problems.*

Ingredients Serves 2 to 4

- ➤ 1 large leek, trimmed and top layers removed
- ➤ 10 oz. sprouts, peeled and trimmed
- ➤ 2 tbsp. double cream
- ➤ 2 knobs of butter
- ➤ salt and pepper

Instructions

- ❖ Using the slicing tool on a food processor, shred the leeks and sprouts, alternatively slice them very, very finely.
- ❖ Heat butter in a large frying pan, when it stops sizzling add the sprouts and leeks.
- ❖ Turn heat down and gently fry for 15 minutes.
- ❖ Add double cream, season well, heat through and serve

10 Rosemary Roast Sweet Potatoes

Sweet potatoes are lower on the glycemic index than brown potatoes but can be used in much the same way: baked, boiled, roasted and mashed. They combine perfectly with the fragrance of rosemary. This dish is a great accompaniment for poultry and vegetarian dishes.

> *Health Bite*
>
> *Sweet potatoes are high in vitamins A, B and C, and are an extremely rich source of beta-carotene, and are high in fiber.*

Ingredients

- ➢ 2 large sweet potatoes, peeled and chopped into 2-inch cubes
- ➢ 2 tsp dried rosemary
- ➢ 2 tbsp. olive oil
- ➢ sea salt and freshly ground black pepper

Instructions

- ❖ Place potatoes in a bowl, pour over olive oil and shake around to ensure all potatoes are evenly coated.
- ❖ Sprinkle on rosemary, salt and pepper.
- ❖ Spread out on a baking tray and bake for 40 to 45 minutes.

11 Tomato Sauce

So simple to make! Great for the carnivore or vegetarian!

> *Health Bite*
>
> *Tomatoes are rich in antioxidants like beta-carotene and lycopene, as well as vitamins C and E. They are great for cancer protection, skin and fertility problems.*

Ingredients

- ➢ 1 medium onion, diced
- ➢ 1 tbsp. oil
- ➢ 3 cloves of garlic peeled and crushed
- ➢ ½ fresh red chili, deseeded
- ➢ 1 tin (440g) plum tomatoes or passata
- ➢ 2 tsp dark unrefined sugar
- ➢ 1 heaped tsp gluten-free stock
- ➢ 1 tsp dried oregano or basil (fresh leaves may be used instead)
- ➢ salt and pepper to taste

Instructions

- ❖ Heat oil and soften onions on a low heat, when softened add chili and garlic for a minute before adding the rest of ingredients.
- ❖ Bring to boil then simmer for 30 mins on lowest heat possible.

❖ Check seasoning then using a hand blender or food processor to blend.

12 Stuffing

This recipe is very similar to the original, and if you don't tell those who aren't gluten or wheat-free, they won't know the difference!

> *Health Bite*
>
> *Sage is rich in volatile oils. It stimulates production of bile, making it great for digestion, especially of fats. Good for menstrual problems and chest infections.*

Ingredients

- ➢ 1 large brown onion chopped and cooked (either in microwave for 2 to 3 minutes or steamed till soft)
- ➢ 2 cups of breadcrumbs (toast wheat-free bread, allow to cool then pulse in a blender)
- ➢ 2 tbsp. dried sage
- ➢ 1 large egg
- ➢ salt and pepper
- ➢ knob of butter melted

Instructions

- ❖ Blend onion in food processor or with hand blender until mushy. Add in all ingredients, season well and mix together.
- ❖ If mixture appears to be too thick add splash of warm water till consistency is like regular stuffing.

❖ Either tip into baking dish or roll into small balls and bake for 20 to 25 minutes in a medium hot oven.

Serving Suggestion: Serve as you would regular stuffing, with chicken or vegetarian protein dishes.

13 Bone Broth

Bone broth is basically stock but made with big bones that you can get from your local butcher (make sure they are from grass-fed cattle).

This broth can be enjoyed on its own or used as stock in sauces and stews.

> *Health Bite*
>
> *Bone broth is packed with minerals that boost the immune system and collagen which helps line and heal the gut.*

Ingredients

- ➢ 2-3 kg of big bones (also works with chicken carcasses)
- ➢ ½ cup white vinegar
- ➢ 2 onions sliced in half
- ➢ 3 carrots, with skins on, scrubbed (if not organic peel the carrots)
- ➢ 3 sticks of celery halved
- ➢ A handful of fresh herbs and peppercorns
- ➢ 2 pints of water or enough to cover ingredients in pot

Instructions

- ❖ Simply pop all the ingredients into a slow cooker or Crok pot, cover with water and simmer on a low heat for 18 to 48 hours.
- ❖ Keep topping up the water levels as needed.
- ❖ Remove and discard the bones, veg and herbs and your broth is ready to eat.

❖ You can divide up into individual portions, pour in freezer bags and freeze.

Section 3

14

Let Nature Heal You

An easy way to reset and rebalance is to get outdoors as often as possible. In fact, for those who are Sensitive, spending time outdoors is near essential.

A stroll through a beautiful woodland, over a grassy meadow or near a natural-flowing stream is not only uplifting but also grounding. It's not by chance Empaths love being outdoors. Their inner-Knowing guides them towards the Earth's natural healing power, to harness its energy.

Spending time in Nature is uplifting for all humans, but to the Sensitive it activates a special kind of magic. It removes impurities from the energy field and quietens a busy, stressed mind. Even sitting in your garden listening to the birds sing, whilst eyeing over the vegetation, has a clearing and calming influence. Whatever the season, it serves the Empath to get outdoors, especially in denser wooded areas.

Woods and forests are as close to healing energy temples as you can get. Trees are powerful and majestic, but few pay little notice to them or their magnificence. Just gazing upon the greenery of a tree has an instant soothing effect, allowing you to experience a release of pent-up emotions you may not realize you had.

The Japanese believe so much in the power of Nature's healing that they developed a health program called Shinrin-Yoku.

Shinrin-Yoku basically means spending more time around trees. It is also known as forest bathing. The idea is to spend a time of quiet contemplation in densely wooded areas. Not jogging, hiking or expending energy, but just drinking in the natural vibrations of Nature. The Japanese found, through scientific studies, that forest bathing has numerous benefits on the physical and psychological. And they discovered it was not just down to the fresh air.

Trees emit oils called phytoncides, which act as protection from germs and insects. These oils also help build a strong immune system. It was also noted that by being in forests, heart rate and blood pressure lowered and stress hormones were significantly reduced. Forest bathing is also known to reduce depression whilst increasing energy.

Green is the color of the heart chakra, and by connecting to Nature you activate the power of your heart, which helps heal and clear your energy field.

As already discussed, the aura is constantly under stress. A poor diet, worry, alcohol, stimulants, medications and other people's energy, weaken the aura, making it permeable. This is bad news. A leaky energy field not only lets energy out but also allows too much external energy in: in the way of other people's negative energy, thought forms and emotions.

Being in Nature helps build a more resilient energy field. This goes a long way to keeping the Empath healthy, grounded and protected.

Here are some more benefits of spending time in Nature:

- Better Sleep
- Reduction of inflammation
- Energy increasing
- Normalizes circadian rhythms
- Relieves muscle tension and headache
- Improves hormone related symptoms
- Speeds healing
- Protects the body from electro-magnetic frequencies (EMF)
- Reduces snoring

After regularly spending time in nature, you notice the energy picked up off others does not affect you in the same way. It seems to bounce off (if only for a short period). Anytime is the perfect time to get outdoors, and if you want to get double the benefits why not try Earthing at the same time?

The Earth's powerful healing energy is something I take for granted or forget about, especially whilst my feet are swathed in toasty socks and sturdy rubber-soled shoes. Grounding with the Earth is also known as Earthing and is a quick powerful way to harness the Earth's power.

Earthing has gone from being a somewhat 'woo-woo New Age trend' to being a well-researched practice, with a number of proven beneficial health benefits. From the perspective of being an Empath, I have found Earthing has some of the following positive benefits:

- Decreases Empath fatigue
- Reduces EMF (electrical magnetic frequencies caused by televisions, computers, mobile phones, etc.). EMF disrupts bioelectrical functions, often leaving the Empath wired or energetically open.
- Helps clear unwanted energy picked up from others.
- Calms the mind. Its grounding effects helps pull us out of our heads and reduces repetitive thoughts.
- Charges us with vibrant energy and positive feelings.
- Contributes to building a more resilient energy field, which helps repel other people's energy.
- In combination with meditation, helps balance the chakras.
- Helps calm the emotions.

The Science Bit

Studies show, the Earth's negative charge can help stabilize internal bioelectrical functions which helps prevent disease and also offers pain relief. We are electrical beings and our bodies produce positive charges, which are harmful in excess. The Earth's abundant free electrons produce a negative charge which works in being counteractive.

According to scientific theory, when Earthing, we absorb an abundance of negatively charged electrons which prove to have an immediate physiological impact. The electrons have the effect of being anti-inflammatory, antioxidative and beneficial to regulating the body's circadian rhythms.

An article published in 'The Journal of Environmental and Public Health' stated the many benefits of Earthing. Their research showed the following were all improved by the act of regular Earthing:

- Sleep
- PMS
- Immune system activity and response
- Hypertension
- Chronic muscular and joint pain
- Asthma
- Energy levels
- Stress
- Arthritis
- Osteoporosis

Researchers believe most health benefits are derived from Earthing's anti-inflammatory effect. By the premise that wherever there is illness there is also inflammation, to reduce inflammation will also reduce disease.

As long as we have a skin on earth connection, by walking, standing, sitting or lying on the ground (grass, earth or beach) it reconnects us with the Earth's powerful energy. Easy to do in the summer, not so much in the cold and wet winter months. If you find Earthing beneficial but cannot get outdoors during the winter, a grounding pad, which harnesses the benefits of Earth's electrons, can be used.

Earthing makes you feel alive and refreshed and is great for staying 'grounded', which is so desperately needed in these trying times.

15

8 Ways to Stop Overwhelm

Emotional overload affects everyone differently; some much worse than others. It can cause distress and misery, and triggers thoughts that keep us awake at night and darken our moods for days.

When we change the diet, periods of overwhelm become less and less. But we are still human and we will still have days where we get peopled or just overwhelmed by the world. And for those such times we have the following quick-fixes.

1: Five second countdown: If the overwhelm you are experiencing has caused your thoughts to become erratic and negative, use the five second countdown. Simply count back from five to one, then take some deep breaths and use positive affirmations such as: 'I am empowered and uplifted', and allow yourself to fill with gratitude. This has an uplifting effect and helps takes your mind off negative repetitive thoughts.

2: Eat a small amount of chocolate: I say small amount because large amounts have the opposite effect (I discovered this the delicious way, by devouring too much).

Chocolate can transform and uplift the mood in an instant. Containing compounds which promote happiness, chocolate is the go-to food when you have been emotionally or energetically overwhelmed. Keep it on hand for when you need a quick-fix, as it releases serotonin. (Serotonin is a neurotransmitter, produced after eating chocolate.)

In my opinion, milk chocolate works better than dark, as the dark stuff contains a higher amount of caffeine. But this is something you can experiment with.

Most chocolate contains refined sugar, which is a big no-no, but you can now buy it made from unrefined sugar stevia or xylitol. Eat between two to four small squares of chocolate washed down with a pint of cool water.

3: Temple hold: Place two to three fingers on either side of the temples (between the eyebrows and hairline) and hold for as long as needed.

This simple technique helps break the repetitive thoughts that are triggered from emotional pain. It also blocks the dense feelings they cause…. I'm not sure why this method works but it does. (I suspect it's because it activates the acupressure points and soothes parts of the brain responsible for emotions.) It is great to do at bedtime when emotional overwhelm turns into rampant thoughts that keep us awake. Taking some calming conscious breaths at the same time further helps.

4: Short bursts of high intensity exercise: A mini power walk, a short run, dynamic yoga moves, dance routines or skipping, etc. helps burn

off raging emotions. I'm talking about very doable bursts of exercise that last between one to five minutes. Performing short bursts of high intensity exercise releases endorphins into the body which block the pain transmission signals and produce euphoric feelings that lift the entire system (See Fundamentals of Exercise).

A great exercise I do, when I have been emotionally fired-up, is the plank. Because it is a challenging move, that activates all the muscles in the body.

Maintaining it for just thirty seconds is often all it takes to blast out the negative emotions that cause overwhelm.

There is a variation of the plank to do whatever your fitness level, from beginners and beyond. You will find plenty of excellent instructional videos on YouTube to get you started.

Whatever exercise you choose, as your mini blast, make sure to do something that makes you feel uncomfortable and your muscles burn. (The saying 'fight fire with fire' springs to mind here).

5: Inhale lavender: When an essential oil, such as lavender, is inhaled through the nose, the cells that line the nasal passages, send messages to the limbic system in the brain, via the olfactory senses, to relax. Lavender's aroma has the ability to instantly relax both body and mind and soothe emotions.

6: Sing or chant: This is not always something we want to do when feeling low, but singing lifts the moods and has an uplifting effect. Singing raises our vibration and stops emotional overwhelm in its tracks. There is a reason song is used in a place of worship, because it lifts the energy. Anyone can sing, hum or

chant. Just make sure it is an uplifting song and not one that stokes up painful memories. Try it and see.

7: Salt: Most already know of the amazing healing properties of salt. It clears negative energies and helps protect us from absorbing them. By adding it to the bath or using salt as a body scrub before and after venturing into peopled places, it helps keep us protected from unwanted energy (it also keeps the skin silky smooth and in tiptop condition). For best results, chose unrefined organic salt. Pink Himalayan rock salt is best.

8: Breath-work: The breath is a powerful tool that most take for granted. The way we feel affects the way we breathe, as can the way we breathe affect the way we feel. Certain breathing techniques work wonders, not only for the way we feel but also for protection to peoples' energy. A great one to use is alternate nostril breathing. Breath-work can also be used pre and post exposure to people's energy. See chapter 8 for instructions.

16

10 Essential Oils to Re-Balance

The value of essential oils has been known for more than 6000 years. Renowned not only for their amazing healing properties and their ability to bring energetic balance back to the body and mind, essential oils also promote emotional wellbeing.

Essential oils are composed of tiny molecules which are easily penetrated by the body. When the essences are inhaled, they enter the body via the cells that line the nasal passages. The cells then send messages to the limbic system in the brain. The limbic system controls our emotions; it also controls the major functions of the body. When messages, from the essential oils, are interpreted by the limbic system it then passes the information on to the rest of the body in the way of healing instructions. In their response, the oils are able to heal and balance both the physical body and emotions at the same time.

If you have used essential oils, you will be familiar with their incredible calming and stabilizing qualities, and if you haven't, now is the time to try them for yourself.

Although the following essential oils have many physically therapeutic benefits, I am mainly listing their energetic and emotional balancing qualities. These oils help soothe the emotions and lift the moods.

1. Basil: Ideal as a nerve tonic, basil lifts fatigue, anxiety and depression. Basil is both relaxing and uplifting. Great to use a few drops in a fragrancer as a mood lifter.

2. Chamomile: Known for its sedative and anti-inflammatory benefits, chamomile is an excellent sleep-aid and helps balance the hormones. It's good to add a few drops on your pillow at night or add to a bath (with a carrier oil).

3. Frankincense: This oil has an uplifting effect and aids concentration by clearing the mind of cluttering thoughts (also known to retain youth and smooth wrinkles... always good to know). Frankincense is excellent to use when you need a clear head for work.

4. Geranium: Unusually, geranium is both sedative and uplifting and invaluable for treating depression and nervous tension. Geranium is great to use when you've been 'peopled' and need to rebalance (also great for skin).

5. Jasmine: Is a mood enhancer, helps balance the emotions, lifts anxiety and depression (also known to be an aphrodisiac).

6. Lavender: Extraordinarily versatile. If you are going to get any essential oil lavender is the one to have. Its sedative and tonic effects make lavender an amazing balancer for the emotional body. The aroma has the ability to instantly relax both body and mind, and clear the negative energy that may have travelled home with you. (Also, anti-fungal, antibacterial, antiseptic and more.)

7. Neroli: Another great oil to use if you have been out in busy public places. An excellent sedative, anti-depressant and re-balancer, neroli counters shock, anxiety and hysteria. It is a great sleep aid and brings about calm to the energetic body.

8. Rose: This is an all-round mood enhancer and general tonic. Rose helps balance the hormones and will clear a muggy head and mental fatigue.

9. Clary Sage: Having both uplifting and relaxing qualities and is known for its sedative and euphoric effects, clary sage is good for insomnia, anxiety and depression, it also helps balance the hormones.

10. Ylang-Ylang: A great relaxer (if used sparingly can get a bit heady and overpowering if too much is used), ylang ylang is highly recommended for anxiety, depression and insomnia.

With the exception of lavender, never use essential oils directly on the skin, always dilute with a carrier oil (e.g. almond, rapeseed or olive oil). Use sparingly. Essential oils are incredibly concentrated. A few drops are generally all that is needed.

There are many ways to use essential oils: Add a couple of drops (with carrier oil) into your bath, use with fragrancers, add a few drops to a cup of water put in a spray bottle and use as a room spray, add a drop or two onto the pooled wax on a candle, add to your body and facial oils, dab on a handkerchief or pillow.

Store your oils in a cool, dark place.

Conclusion

When we become stronger in the mind, body and spirit, the way we show up in the world completely changes. Life becomes easier, less painful and more rewarding. We gain clarity and insight of what our journey is about and we become keen to walk it.

I know what Sensitive suffering is all about and although I know pain serves a purpose that can push us towards a higher path, it is completely unnecessary to endure prolonged anguish.

You have to remember your worth and know you have purpose and meaning. It is time to reconnect with yourself and the way you do that is by making inner-changes. Clean up your body and mind. Remove that which keeps you down or weakens you. Find your inner fire and shine your light. You are extraordinary and here for a purpose. You know you are, you can feel it. Remove your shackles and allow your true Self to emerge.

You have the power!

Diane Kathrine ©

Further Reading and References

Wheat Belly: William Davis. MD

The Grain Brain: David Perlmutter. MD

Dr. Christine Zioudrou's papers on opioid peptides and other similar articles:
www.ncbi.nlm.nih.gov/pubmed/372181

Blood Sugar Blues: Miryam Enrlich Williamson

The Blood Sugar Solution: Dr Mark Hyman

The New Optimum Nutrition Bible: Patrick Holford

Prescription for Nutritional Healing: Phyllis A. Balch CNC

The Encyclopedia of Healing Foods: Michael Murray N.D.

Autoimmune Fix: Tom O'Bryan

The Highly Sensitive Person: Elaine N. Aron

Other Books by Diane Kathrine

7 Secrets of the Sensitive – *Harness the Empath's Hidden Power!*

Empath Power – *Grounding Healing and Protection for Life!*

The Empath Awakening – *Navigating Life in the Sensitive Lane*

How to Heal Leaky Aura *A Guide for Empaths*

Traits of an Empath *Understand Who You Are*

Become the Super-Empowered Empath You Were Born to Be! *Rediscover the Secret to Transform Your Life (Release date 30 December 2018)*

Diane blogs at: www.theknowing1.wordpress.com

CPSIA information can be obtained
at www.ICGtesting.com
Printed in the USA
BVHW041123051221
623269BV00015B/1360